Dave DeWitt's
CHILE
TRIVIA

Sunbelt Media
Los Ranchos, New Mexico
www.SunbeltMedia.net

Printed in the U.S.A.
Book design by Lois Manno

Library of Congress Cataloging-in-Publication Data

DeWitt, Dave.
Dave Dewitt's chile trivia : weird, wacky factoids for curious chileheads / by Dave DeWitt and Lois Manno.
p. cm.
Includes bibliographical references and index.
ISBN 978-1-936744-00-8 (pbk. : alk. paper)
1. Hot peppers--Miscellanea. 2. Cooking (Hot peppers)
I. Manno, Lois (Lois S.) II. Title.
SB307.P4D495 2012
641.3'384--dc23
2012000204

Dave DeWitt's
CHILE TRIVIA

Weird, Wacky Factoids
For Curious Chileheads

Dave DeWitt and Lois Manno

Published by Sunbelt Media,
an Imprint of Rio Grande Books

This book is dedicated to the memory of Lord Harris. Find out who he is in Chapter 14.

Contents

Preface

From Dave DeWitt:

I've written 5,738,612 words about chile peppers during my hot and spicy career, and that's just an approximation. The ubiquitous "they" call me "The Pope of Peppers" but I'm more into chile messes than masses. Of course, I'm enormously grateful for all the respect and adulation this title implies and am duly honored. Now, where's the cash?

Maybe this book will generate it, since it's my most thorough compilation of interesting chile pepper trivia to date. Much of this material was buried in my archives, and it took Lois and me several weeks to collect it, edit it, recover from the humor hangover, and get it ready for publication. In addition, we updated all the references and added brand-new material to keep up with current spicy trends.

From Lois Manno:

My relationship with spicy food and Pope Dave began about 20 years ago, when he was editor of the original *Chile Pepper* magazine and I was its art director. As one of the truly addicted, several feet of shelf space in my tiny kitchen is reserved for my favorite fiery products, and I eat something spicy at least once a day.

Dave definitely did the heavy lifting on this project. My contribution was in updating archival material that was out of date, finding the newest info about chile trends, etc. I also had the pleasure of taking text that was already absurd and interesting, and "amping it up" a bit. I designed the book as well.

Dave really understated the length of time it took to compile this vast amount of trivia. It reminds me of the artist who, when asked how long it took for him to make a particular work of art, replied "It took three weeks to do the painting, and thirty years to learn how."

Introduction

They Call Me
"The Pope of Peppers"

I wasn't born loving chile peppers. In fact, I didn't taste one until I was twenty-eight years old. I grew up in northern Virginia, not quite the center of chile pepper activity. My first taste was in the Bahamas—my wife-to-be (the second one), Luci, and I were on a Windjammer cruise where the cook prepared and served a traditional island dish, Conch Salad. It was spiced up with goat peppers, the common name there for the *Capsicum chinense* species, which includes the habanero, 'Scotch bonnet', and even 'Bhut Jolokia'. The salad was hot, but not overwhelming. I liked it, but promptly forgot about it after the trip.

Flash-forward two years to 1974—Luci and I were visiting her parents in Albuquerque. It was time to Burn Out the Gringo, a New Mexico ritual designed to teach Easterners a lesson about the spicy, chile-drenched foods of the Land of Enchantment. For my ritual, the torture food was green chile stew. *Very hot* (for me) green chile stew, the kind that made my bald spot sweat (it's more than just a spot now) and my body to start producing hiccups. I ate half a bowl and the other dinner guests were impressed. I finished the bowl and asked the server for more…I passed the test and was hooked.

Then we moved to New Mexico and my life changed forever. I started my writing career. Luci left to become a cowgirl, I found my current (and final) wife Mary Jane, and we've been together ever since. I also met my coauthor Nancy Gerlach, who was a recipe developer and registered dietitian. We began to write the book that launched it all, *The Fiery Cuisines*, which St. Martin's Press published in 1984. Three years later, Nancy, Robert Spiegel, and I launched *Chile Pepper* magazine, and in 1988 Mary Jane and I founded the first National Fiery Foods Show. We were on a roll, and it's never slowed down.

As I write this in December 2011, I'm working on book number forty-four. Or maybe forty-five—I forget. The interest worldwide in chile peppers and fiery foods is still growing, as amazing as that may be. Now the hot stuff is loved all over Europe—the last citadel of bland to fall to the chiles' onslaught on the world of food. With Sweden producing hot sauce, with a variety of chile having received official name recognition in France, with chilli festivals hugely popular in England, and with farms growing superhot chiles in Italy, my work on chile peppers is complete and I'm retiring to write about tofu and other GMO delights.

Just kidding. Every time I think that there are no more books on chiles I can possibly write, someone thinks of one and assigns it to me. This time it was Barbe Awalt of LPD Press who thought of trivia, and knowing me pretty darned well, she had a hunch that I had a treasure trove of trivia about chiles and fiery foods. She was dead-on, and here it is. This book is totally assembled from my archives of a quarter-century or more of writing about hot stuff, so it sorta, kinda tells an informal history of the entire spicy movement.

It's been a fun ride and I hope this is a fun read.

Dave in a peri peri field in South Africa. Photo by Mary Jane Wilan

Dave DeWitt's Chile Trivia

A Note on Usage

You Say Chili, I Say Chile, They Say Chilli

A great deal of discussion and controversy has erupted over the terminology of the Capsicum family in English. There are hundreds—if not thousands—of terms for the pods in languages from all over the world, so it is curious that the following terms have been debated with such passion.

Ají This word, from the Arawaks of the West Indies, was transferred to South America by the Spanish and became the general term there for Capsicums of all varieties, but specifically the species *baccatum*. It is used in South America, as the word *chile* is used in Central America and Mexico.

Capsicum From the Greek *kapto*, to bite, this is the botanical name for the genus and the one preferred by the scientific community. We would assume that there would be little controversy here, except for two drawbacks. First, the term is unfamiliar to most people; and second, the term "capsicum" specifically means bell pepper in the United Kingdom, Singapore and other English-speaking parts of Southeast Asia.

Pepper Of course, we know that Christopher Columbus used the Spanish term *pimiento*, which means black pepper, to describe the Capsicums. According to some writers, this means that the word pepper should never be used for the Capsicums because of the confusion with black pepper. However, in English the word pepper is either plural ("give me some peppers") or modified by either chile or chili, so the possibility of confusing green pods with black peppercorns is remote.

Chile This is the Mexican Spanish term for Capsicums, supposedly derived from *chilli* (see below). It is also used in New Mexico as both a noun and an adjective before the word pepper. It is spelled with an "e" to avoid confusion with chili, meaning chili con carne. Surprisingly, many newspapers in the U.S. have changed the spelling from chili to chile over the past decade. This is probably because of the popularity of *Chile Pepper* magazine and the many cookbooks using the spelling that have been published.

Chili This is the Anglicized version of *chile* that is probably the most popular spelling in the U.S., Germany, and Canada. It is also both a noun and an adjective when followed by pepper. It is also the short-ened version of chili con carne, the dish with Capsicums, meat, spices, and occasionally beans, so there can be confusion in a headline such as "Fred Jones Wins Chili Contest." Did he win for his pods from his garden or his bowl of red?

Chilli Pepper expert Jean Andrews believes that the proper English term is *chilli*. This is also the British spelling for hot peppers, but her argument goes back to the Aztecs. She writes that the Nahuatl language spelling, as transliterated by Dr. Francisco Hernandez (1514-1578), was *chilli*. She observes: "That Spanish spelling was later changed to *chile* by the Spanish-speaking Mexicans, and 'chili' in the United States. *Chilli* is the name most used by English speaking people throughout the world." This may be so, but the question arises as to the original transliteration. When translating a non-written word into a written language, all kinds of lingustic problems can occur, which is why we call the city Beijing instead of Peking now. If Hernandez was correct, the proper pronunciation of the word would be "chee-yee" because the double L in Spanish is pronounced like an English Y. Since no one pronounces the words chile, chili, or chilli this way, why is the spelling so important?

Chile (or Chili) Peppers Depending on your point of view, this term is either redundant or extremely precise. It is used to distinguish the plants and the pods from dishes made with them, but purists object to both: using chile or chili as an adjective and to using the word pepper.

Conclusion The many spellings and the syntax of the words used to describe the Capsicum genus will never be standardized. This is because—and I'm not being being flip—no one really cares outside of academia, and even the experts there disagree. Languages evolve, and because of the increasing popularity of Capsicums, the terms to describe them are better known and there is less chance of confusion. And to paraphrase William Shakespeare, what's in a name? A chile pepper by any other name would still have heat.

Some typical chile pod shapes. Illustration by Lois Manno

A Note on Usage

A peppersauce pinup girl. Digital image by Lois Manno

Dave DeWitt's Chile Trivia

Part I

It's Your Chilehead Life

Chiles are a lifestyle. It's an urban cowboy idea of bravado. You have a sense of machismo without running around with a gun rack in the back of your truck. There's got to be a way of proving one's bravado. Chiles are one way of doing that. Chiles will become more popular everywhere. People want—and need—a sense of the exotic.

—Coyote Cafe founder Mark Miller

The guys from Fire on the Ridge messing around at the 2010 Fiery Foods & BBQ Show.
Photo by Wes Naman

Dave DeWitt's Chile Trivia

Chapter 1

Chiles in Modern Culture

I'm the perfect example of someone who takes chile peppers so seriously that they take over his life. By serious, I mean I've been dedicated to them for decades, but they're certainly not lacking in humor, as this book shows in agonizing detail. The only neckties I own have chile peppers on them. There are eight chile-related pieces of art in our kitchen. All of our vacations are taken in areas that grow chiles or brew beer. I grow a modest chile garden myself every year, but we can't eat them all so I give them away. I have donated hundreds of chile-related books, articles, photos, and manuscripts to the New Mexico State University Library, where they will live on after I depart to the Big Pod in the Sky.

I don't have a hot sauce collection. I don't wear chile-emblazoned underpants or jock straps. I don't put hot sauce in my coffee. I will not attempt to eat a superhot chile or swallow a superhot sauce. I did donate white bread and milk to the Chile Pepper Addiction Recovery Center next to my house, but the patients flamed me on Facebook. I got into trouble once by writing that chile peppers were as easy to grow as tomatoes. Or maybe it was the other way around. Then I really got into trouble when I wrote that marijuana was easier to grow than either of those, not that I've actually tried it.

However, it does seem to me that some of the stories in this chapter may have been marijuana-influenced.

Chile peppers are the biggest food craze to hit the American palate since...well, since chocolate. True, garlic and barbecue have had their moments, and even their newsletters, but nothing like the spate of cookbooks, press hype, mail-order purveyors, posters, Christmas lights, and other collectibles that has followed in the wake of chilemania.

—Best-selling culinary writer John Thorne

It's politically correct thrill-seeking, in which we can publicly engage—on a date, a game of I'll show you mine if you show me yours, and with friends or siblings, open challenge without warfare...It's the dining room equivalent of bungee-jumping.

—Food writer Jennifer Farley

Do Men Like Spicy Food More Than Women Do?

When it comes to eating chile, there's no proven biological link between gender and preference. If anything, blame the misconception that hot peppers are a "guy thing" on Madison Avenue. Whether they're marketed as such or not, we all tend to think of everyday items, including food and beverages, as one gender or the other, says James Wilkie, a doctoral candidate in marketing at Northwestern University in Illinois. According to Wilkie, humans instinctively categorize other individuals as male or female, but they don't stop there. He says, "we tend to almost reflexively apply it to things that perhaps it's not relevant to apply it to." In a 2010 study, Wilkie examined how gender preconceptions affect people's food choices. Men, more than women, he found, tend to be more concerned about choosing foods that conform to gender norms. For instance, they often choose rib-eye steaks, gravy and dishes described as "hearty" over supposedly feminine foods like salads. So screw the salad, girls...hot sauce isn't just for guys.

Red or Green?

In 1999 the New Mexico State Legislature enacted a memorial making "Red or Green?" the official New Mexico State Question. That's right, your state can have an official question. How's that for an example of distinguished political statesmanship? Just to complicate matters, there's a third answer to what appears to be a two-answer question.

If you want both red and green chile on your enchiladas, the correct answer to "Red or Green?" is…Christmas!

How Is A Chile's Heat Level Measured?

There are two main methods used for determining how hot a chile pepper is: the Scoville Organoleptic Test uses human testers, who taste a series of chile samples. The samples are diluted further and further until the tasters can't sense any more heat. It's a bit subjective because tasters can have varying degrees of sensitivity to capsaicinoids. This method was developed by Wilbur Scoville, an American pharmacist, in 1912. Hence the name, "Scoville Scale."

The most accurate method for measuring chile heat is high-performance liquid chromatography (HPLC), which is used almost exclusively these days. No human tasters are involved; instead, the chemicals responsible for heat are extracted from ground samples, and measured by machine. It's more expensive, but also much more precise and efficient. The New Mexico State University Chile Breeding and Genetics Program has analyzed more than 5,000 samples using this method and has found it to be extremely reliable.

Chile Eating Contests Hit A Crazy New Level

Braulio Ramirez earned the title of Jalapeño King at the 1992 Jalapeño Festival in Laredo, Texas by consuming an astonishing 141 jalapeños in fifteen minutes. He barely beat out Jed Donahue, who consumed more than 150 jalapeños but was disqualified for vomiting. Compare that to the 2009 Guinness World Record set by a 28-year-old Indian woman, who ate 51 superhot ghost peppers in two minutes. To underscore the quantum leap in pep-

Professor Wilbur Scoville, the Once and Future King of Chilehead Geeks, invented the Scoville Heat Scale in 1912.

It's Your Chilehead Life

per-eating that this represents, consider this—the average jalapeño pepper registers at 3,500 to 8,000 Heat Units on the Scoville Heat Scale. A ghost pepper registers well over 1 million Units. That means you'd need to eat 200 jalapeños to ingest the same amount of capsaicin contained in one ghost pepper.

Chile Eating Contestants Feel the Burn
The following list of physiological responses have been reported by people participating in chile pepper-eating contests:
Vomiting
Numbness to tongue and mouth
Temporary loss of eyesight
Light-headedness
Stomach pains requiring hospitalization
Nosebleed
Excessive sweating
Panting
It's recommended that those who participate in chile-eating contests make sure they have plenty of rolls of toilet paper stashed in the freezer for the morning after.

But Will It Work on Sharks?
Capsaicin has been recommended as a preventative for biofouling, which is the technical term for the growth of barnacles and other marine organisms. Anti-fouling paint is made for boat bottoms to control this pesky biological buildup. Capsaicin is registered by the Environmental Protection Agency (EPA) as a bird, animal, and insect repellent. In 1991, it was reclassified by the EPA as a biochemical pesticide. Boat owners have been known to add a bottle of Tabasco® sauce to a gallon of anti-fouling paint before applying it to the hulls of their vessels. I hear they did the same on the *USS Bloody Mary*.

Fiery Fast Food Takes Flight
The combination of chile peppers with fast food is a match made in heaven. The marketing staff at Kentucky Fried Chicken found this out when the company introduced Hot Wings in an attempt to capitalize on the popularity of "buffalo wings." Fiery foods fans flew in to consume the wings in such hordes that the company suspended its national advertising campaign because sales were running fifty percent above projections.

Not to be outdone, the unflappable folks at Wendy's came out with several spicy additions to the menu, spicy chipotle boneless "wings." If you've ever considered what would be involved in deboning a chicken wing, you'd realize that what would be left after the process would be a teensy lump of shredded meat, hardly enough to make a mouthful. The boneless "wings" probably contain no wing meat at all, and are simply elongated chicken nuggets made from breast meat.

We think the confusion between wings and breasts can be traced directly to the hugely successful Victoria's Secret lingerie marketing plan, which features buxom models sporting enormous feathery faux wings while wearing skimpy underwear (quick, somebody bring the smelling salts!).

Is Pepper Spray Deadly?
It depends on who you ask. The National Institute of Justice had this to say about pepper spray: "Though generally assumed to be safe and effective, the consequences of the use of pepper spray, as with any use of force, can never be predicted with certainty. While the research does not and cannot prove that pepper spray will never be a contributing factor in the death of a subject resisting arrest, it seems to confirm that pepper spray is a reasonably safe and effective tool for law enforcement officers to use when confronting uncooperative or combative subjects." According to a 1995 Southern California ACLU study, twenty-six deaths occurred among people pepper sprayed by police between 1993 and 1995. In the mid-'90s, state officials were report-

Pepper spray is becoming increasingly popular as a form of crowd control. Too bad nobody knows how dangerous it is. Here Seattle police apply pepper spray to protestors in 1999. Photo by Steve Kaiser

ing 5,000 sprayings annually, a leap from nearly zero to 15,688 total incidents since 1992. In fact, Defense Technology Corporation, which *manufactures* pepper spray, wrote that "…little or nothing is known about the health risk or toxicity of pepper spray…"

But that doesn't stop people from using it. In 2011 campus police at UC Davis lavished it on protesters as they sat peacefully on the ground during an Occupy Wall Street event. Then a woman at a Southern California Wal-Mart busted it out on her fellow shoppers late Thursday night so she could get dibs on an Xbox 360 for Black Friday. Why, it's getting so you can't go into a hostile mob standing in line at Starbucks without a good chance of catching a healthy dose of the stuff.

North Carolina police trainer John Schneider had this to say about capsicum pepper spray: "Whatever your problems were in this world before you were sprayed, you won't think about them for the next thirty or forty minutes."

Lipstick or Pepper Spray?

The Safetygirl website sells pepper spray canisters that look like tubes of lipstick and come in an array of "fashion colors." Does it really make sense to disguise your pepper spray as something you normally would smear on your mouth? This description appears on the site: *Designed just for women, this attractive lipstick case is sure to deceive and ward off potential attackers. Pretend you need to freshen your lipstick and POW!* We can see it now: "Excuse me, Mr. Rapist, could you just hang on for a minute while I touch up my face?"

Police Academy Revisited: Officers Assaulted with Tabasco® Sauce

This is the city: Lebanon, New Hampshire. It's normally a quiet place, but sometimes people get out of control—especially when it concerns state troopers from Vermont. Michael Towne, 20, a cook at a Denny's restaurant, was charged with assault for allegedly spiking two Vermont state troopers' eggs with Tabasco® sauce. If convicted, the penalty would be to two years in jail and a $4,000 fine. Troopers Timothy Clouatre and Michael Manning, who had crossed into New Hampshire for breakfast, complained that the eggs burned their mouths and upset one officer's stomach. They confronted Towne, who claimed that he had not done the spiking on purpose but that the sauce was residue on the grill from an earlier order. The troopers didn't believe him and Towne was arrested. According to police sources, Towne, who reportedly disliked cops, was seen by a witness deliberately dousing the officers' eggs. "We got enough trouble without people screwing around with our food," groused Lebanon police Lt. Ken Gary.

The Darker Side of Chile

Reports in the *San Diego Union-Tribune* on corruption in Mexico's highest political offices and law enforcement agencies have taken a dark turn. Witnesses/victims have claimed they can prove police officers tortured them while they were in custody. One alleged method of torture involved flushing a water/chile powder mixture up the nose. Indians in Peru reputedly snort a mixture of cocaine and ground chile, but that's more like self-punishment.

They Put Chile *Where*?

According to Arturo Lomelí in his book, *El Chile y Otros Picantes*, chile in various forms has been used for torture or punishment since the days before Cortes arrived in Mexico. There are reports that Indians made huge bonfires of chiles so that the smoke would block the path of advancing Spanish conquerors. Lomelí wrote that a form of this technique remains today among Popolacan Indians near Oaxaca when they need to punish disobedient children. Other methods that persist to this day include daubing a chile-and-oil mixture on children's fingers to discourage thumb-sucking, and mixing chile on mothers' nipples to accelerate weaning of a child who nurses too long.

All stops come out with *Chilazo*, a chile fumigant or smoke bomb, used to eliminate rats, insects, and other unwanted pests such as scorpions from Mexican homes. However, Lomeli also documents the longtime use of chile pods to warn off the Evil Eye or to protect newborn babies, in much the same way that Mediterranean cultures use cloves of garlic or other amulets.

You Know You're a Real Chilehead If...

...You consider habaneros to be one of the four basic food groups.

...There are more than thirty opened bottles of hot sauce in your refrigerator.

...Your dog Pepper refuses scraps from the dinner table.

...You consider hot sauce on your oatmeal an intriguing idea.

...You no longer get to cook at family get-togethers.

...You have a bake sale consisting of chile-laced pastries to raise money to go to the Fiery Foods Show.

...You have insured your hot sauce collection for more than what your car is worth.

… Your toilet paper spontaneously combusts after use.

...You know that "chile" denotes peppers and "chili" refers to that brown stuff Texans eat.

Hot Sauce Insurance for Pizza Theft

The crimes occurred at night. A person or persons unknown were raiding the corporate refrigerator at a large insurance company in a major Southwestern city (we can't reveal any names for insurance reasons) and stealing slices of leftover pizza. The cleaning crew was suspected, as were several employees who "worked late." Ace investigator D.S. notified America's Most Wanted and circulated threatening memos around the office that promised demerits to persons apprehended with the purloined pizza— but the snackfood scofflaws persisted to deplete the pizza pantry.

And then D.S. had the hot flash: penalize the pizza pilferer with pungency! From his pantry he plucked the perfect punishment (okay, okay, I'll stop): a bottle of the hottest habanero sauce he had ever tasted.

The next morning he bought a pizza. A bland pizza. Back at the office, with his trusty Swiss Army knife, he carefully cut apart the bottom crust of each slice and slathered the sections with searing sauce! (Sorry.)

D.S. covered the pizza with plastic wrap and placed a note on it that read: "Property of D.S. Do not eat under penalty of impalement." Then he placed it in the refrigerator and went home for the day. The following morning, D.S. found that his pizza was perfect—except for one major bite out the end of one slice. "Aha," declared D.S., "it's a hot pepper payback." The moral of this story is: A pizza saved is a pizza burned.

Why Is There Chile in my Cheetos?

What's behind the rising heat tolerance of American taste buds? Several factors, experts say. Changing demographics—in particular, growing Latin American and Asian populations—are partially responsible for an increase in demand for chile-laden products. Foreign travel, increased availability of once-obscure chile ingredients in grocery stores and more ethnic restaurants mean our palates are becoming more accustomed to hot and spicy foods. At the same time, aging baby-boomers, whose taste buds have become duller as they've gotten older, find they're looking for more of a kick from their dinners. That kick is something also sought by kids growing up taking part in extreme sports during the day and watching shows like "Fear Factor" at night. Enter Fiery Habanero Doritos …

Fire Extinguisher: The Best Cool-Down Method

Debate has raged for years about the most effective antidote for a mouth burning from chile backdraft. Some suggested remedies have included tea, beer, bread, honey, lemon, and the totally ineffective water.

As I described in *The Whole Chile Pepper Book*, studies have shown that dairy products such as milk, cream, sour cream, ice cream, and yogurt are the most effective cool-downs. We knew dairy products worked best, but we didn't know why.

Now we do, thanks to Robert Henken of the Taste and Smell Clinic in Washington, D.C., writing in *The Journal of the American Medical Association*. It's capsaicin, of course, that causes "intense oral burning" when it binds to nerve receptors in the mouth, he says. And it's the protein casein in milk that "acts like a detergent and literally wipes or strips the capsaicin from its receptor site."

The late John Riley, who was editor-publisher of the quarterly journal *Solanaceae*, tested various folk remedies reputed to remove the heat of the capsaicin in chile peppers. In each test, a slice of serrano chile was chewed for one minute, and then one of the remedies was applied. The amount of time until the burning sensation eased was measured and the results were recorded. Ordinary milk was the clear winner.

Remedy	Total Minutes
Rinse the mouth with water only	11
Rinse the mouth with one tablespoon olive oil	10
Drink 1/2 cup heavy fruit syrup	10
Rinse mouth with 1 tablespoon glycerine	8
Drink 1/2 cup milk, rinsing well	7

A Chilehead's Martha Stewart Moment

Got red chile stains on light colored clothing? The cure is washing first and then exposing the stained fabric to several hours of direct (not incidental) sunlight.

But Did it Stain Anybody's Dress?

Former President Bill Clinton, on a visit to Albuquerque, ordered red chile enchiladas and other New Mexican food from Garcia's Kitchen to serve his staff of eighty aboard Air Force One...unfortunately, as the food was being served, the plane hit turbulence over Lubbock, and the red chile was splattered everywhere.

We need a fix of red or green with a side order of endorphins. We get slightly strung out on endorphins, but it's no big deal. It's not like heroin addiction.

—Dr. Frank Etscorn,
inventor of the nicotine patch

Dave DeWitt's Chile Trivia

Chapter 2

Capsaicin and Medical Matters

I have long been fascinated by the growing body of evidence indicating that chile peppers and their derivatives are both a preventative—for maintaining health—and a curing agent for many medical conditions. In researching the book, *The Healing Powers of Peppers* (1998), my coauthors and I analyzed thousands of pages of scientific information. But the most fascinating and hopeful research we did involved interviewing people whose health has been improved by using chile peppers in some form.

Although such testimonials and their anecdotal evidence are generally ignored or dismissed by the medical establishment, I agree with Andrew Weil on the subject. He wrote in *Spontaneous Healing*: "Testimonials are important pieces of evidence. They are not necessarily testimony to the power and value of particular healers and products. Rather, they are testimony to the human capacity for healing. The evidence is incontrovertible that the body is capable of healing itself. By ignoring that, many doctors cut themselves off from a tremendous source of optimism about health and healing."

Anecdotal evidence, because it's not part of established scientific and medical procedure, is often regarded as being "trivial." But in this book, even the medical studies themselves are reduced to trivia, mostly because we usually never hear about them again. The point is that medical scientists are attempting to unravel the secrets of capsaicin, and in doing this they are increasing our knowledge. Eventually this may translate into improved health for us all.

Are Chileheads Really Addicted?

In his 1980 book, *The Marriage of the Sun and Moon*, Dr. Andrew Weil related a story from Santha Rama Rau's book, *The Cooking of India*, where an Indian woman visiting London became ill from the bland food and craved chiles so much that she poured three-quarters of a bottle of Tabasco® sauce, plus sixteen red-hot South American chiles over her omelet before she was satisfied.

This might sound like the behavior of a true addict, but According to Paul Rozin, Ph.D., a psychologist at the University of Pennsylvania who has done extensive research on the acquisition of chile preference, chile does not meet the criteria for true physical addiction, which involves the following symptoms:

Craving: For chile, this exists to a degree, but it never becomes a physical necessity.

Loss of control. Chileheads are always totally in control (sure).

Withdrawal: We miss it, but we don't get sick without it.

Tolerance: We adjust to higher heat levels, but we don't need increasing amounts just to feel normal.

Rozin also says that people who do not like chile do not reverse their preference as the negative taste of chile wears off (which is what happens with addictive substances such as alcohol and nicotine), and conversely, there is no evidence that the preference for chile wears off, even after long periods (weeks to years) of not eating it. Former smokers, for instance, can become ill if they try a cigarette after having not smoked for a certain amount of time.

Additionally, a study at Duke University Medical Center found that in smaller doses, capsaicin and nicotine induce some of the same physiological responses, including irritation, secretion, sneezing, vasodilation, coughing, and peptide release. However in larger, injected doses, capsaicin destroys many of the neurons containing its receptors, while nicotine actually increases the number of nicotine acetylcholine receptor. What this means is that large doses of capsaicin result in the body becoming less responsive to capsaicin, but that large doses of nicotine cause the body to become more responsive to nicotine.

Do Chiles Make You High?

Apparently so. Experimental psychologist Dr. Frank Etscorn posed a theory that the warm afterglow and the constant craving for chile are due to capsaicin triggering the release of the body's natural painkillers. Called endorphins, these "natural opiates" produced by the body are the cause of the so-called runner's high, and are capable of turning a painful experience into a pleasurable one.

To establish a link between capsaicin and endorphins, Etscorn used a drug called naxalone, which can reverse the effects of a heroin overdose by blocking brain receptors that respond to the heroin (these same receptors also respond to endorphins). In one experiment, he had a student eat the hottest jalapeños he could find until his mouth was burning up and perspiration was pouring off his face. The student was then asked to indicate when the pain began to diminish, and was given at that point a naxalone injection, which caused the pain to increase as the endorphins were blocked from the brain. Poor guy; hopefully he at least got an A for his efforts.

The Spicy Inferno

Thirteen shoppers were hospitalized and the Fallbrook Mall in California's San Fernando Valley was evacuated when an irritating cloud of smoke filled the mall. Firefighters searching for the source of the fire finally uncovered the culprit: the blackened remains of cayenne chiles in a frying pan.

It seems that a cook at one of the specialty food restaurants in the mall accidentally burned the peppers while cooking them in hot oil and caused considerable panic. Since the smoke from burning hot chiles was once used as a chemical warfare weapon in pre-Columbian South America, cooks should always exercise caution, especially when working with habaneros and other ultra-hot varieties.

Do Chiles Heal or Hurt You?

Depending on the dose, they can do either. Any doubts about the power of capsaicin should be dispelled after reading the following two news items. Chile-eating contests have now been proven to be dangerous—if not potentially deadly. The *Journal of the American Medical Association* reported that a 23-year-old Israeli man who ate 25 chile peppers in 12 minutes suffered a ruptured duodenal ulcer. He survived because of a quick operation, but the doctors on the case noted "mechanical injury of the duodenal wall, acute hyperacidity, and direct irritation by capsaicin."

On the other hand, capsaicin continues to demonstrate its ability to control pain. According to a report in *Science News*, capsaicin can block a person's ability to feel burn pain without producing numbness. Capsaicin creams are routinely used to help relieve the pain of arthritis. Researchers with Case Western Reserve University examined the use of capsaicin cream in 70 patients with osteoarthritis and 31 with rheumatoid arthritis. After 4 weeks of applying a 0.025% capsaicin cream or placebo to painful knees, the capsaicin patients had significantly more pain relief. Rheumatoid arthritis patients had 57% pain reduction and osteoarthritis patients had 33% pain reduction-both were considered more effective than placebo. These examples vividly demonstrate the two sides of capsaicin: its ability to heal in small doses and hurt in large doses.

Capsaicin: Cancer Cure...Or Cause?

Chemists call it a vanillylamide of dicilenic acid; we call it the chemical that makes chiles hot. Depending on the medical researcher you ask, chiles can be both a cause and potential cure of some forms of cancer. According to one report, capsaicin has been linked to colon cancer through studies conducted among chile pepper eaters in India and Korea. But another study showed that in the liver, capsaicin is transformed into a compound that soaks up chemicals called free radicals, which are thought to cause cancer.

In a 2011 study of potential skin cancer triggers, Researchers at The Hormel Institute, University of Minnesota, treated the skin of mice with a mixture of TPA and DMBA, two powerful and highly toxic tumor-producing chemicals. The mice were virtually guaranteed to develop skin cancer. Some were treated with a mixture of the chemicals plus capsaicin, and some were treated with capsaicin only.

While study results indicated that combining capsaicin with the chemicals "might promote cancer cell survival," the report clearly stated that the control group of mice treated only with capsaicin "… did not induce any skin tumors…" In addition, the study repeatedly cited other research studies in which the anti-cancer properties of capsaicin were solidly demonstrated.

"Some of the chemicals in hot peppers appear to be cancer- causing, but the same ones can protect against cancer," said Peter Gannett of the University of Nebraska Medical Center. "The overall effect depends upon how much you eat." Skeptics insist that the researchers are trying to scare us again with another potential carcinogen, just as they have in the past with the highly exaggerated dangers of coffee, sugar, and cranberries.

One critic calculated that a person would have to consume two pounds of capsaicin to see the effects the Nebraska research suggested. Since we can taste capsaicin in solutions as diluted as one part in one million, there may only be two pounds of capsaicin in the entire annual world crop of chiles!

...And More on the Cancer Question

Two recent studies have shown that capsaicin can kill cancer cells with little or no harmful side effects. The study, which was conducted at

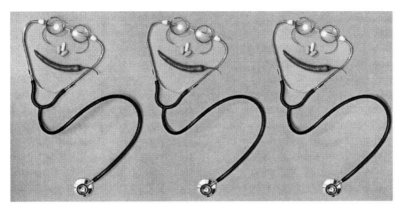

the University of Nottingham in England, shows that capsaicin attacks the mitochondria of cancerous cells, causing them to "switch off" and die without harming surrounding tissue. Mitochondria are organelles (tiny granules of tissue with their own DNA) that live inside the cells of our bodies and convert nutrients into the chemical that feeds our cells with energy. Sounds creepy, but it's true.

The capsaicin was tested on H460 human lung cancer cells, which are recognized as the "gold standard" for anti-cancer drugs. However, they also tested similar compounds on pancreatic cancer cells and found the same effect – the tumor cells died off, leaving the surrounding tissue intact. This is a very exciting result because pancreatic cancer has a five-year survival rate of one percent and is currently one of the most stubborn cancers to treat.

As far as development costs and timescales go, these compounds have already been approved for use in a range of drugs such as skin ointments to treat psoriasis and neuralgia. Converting their use to treat cancer would be much cheaper and faster compared to starting from scratch with a new and unknown compound.

Dr. Timothy Bates, who led the research team, believes that this discovery may explain why people in countries that consume more chile—such as Mexico, India and China—have lower incidences of cancer. One more reason to love the pod!

Hung Over? Eat Chiles!

Mouth dry, stomach somersaulting, head aching… If you've ever had a hangover, these symptoms will sound very familiar. And though everyone is affected differently, and every culture has its own ideas about how to treat ailments, the search for a good hangover cure is worldwide. Some facts are clear across the board: for example, that dehydration, low blood sugar levels, inflammation and stomach irritation all contribute to the "morning after" misery. And so some treatments—like drinking water—are fairly obvious.

But have you ever considered that spicy foods might make the pain go away? Things like curries and chile peppers offer the hung-over masses two welcome areas of relief: chile is a stimulant, so it is likely to provide a temporary pick-me-up, plus it acts as a good decongestant, which will help to reduce the swelling that alcohol causes inside of the nose. So next time you have a big night on the town, prepare yourself some curry for breakfast, or a spicy green chile omelet with Tabasco® on top! Better yet, bite down on a ghost chile and you'll forget all about your hangover. We promise.

A Chile a Day Keeps The Doctor Away

Recent studies show hot peppers can increase blood flow, and thus may prevent blood clots and possibly heart disease in general. Already proven to relieve headaches and sinus inflammation, capsaicin (the "hot" in hot peppers), when ingested, activates the body's circulation dramatically. Unlike drugs with speed-like effects, capsaicin has a natural ability to conduct heat and inhibit nerve receptors that cause pain and swelling, thus promoting circulatory blood flow. Multiple studies on gastrointestinal diseases have found that capsaicin also increases blood flow to the stomach, and stimulates the production of digestive juices. There is even evidence, from a study done on rats, that capsaicin may protect against stomach damage caused by alcohol.

Does Spicing Up Food Help With Dieting?

Diet-conscious chileheads rejoice! A study at Laval University in Quebec, Canada investigated the effects of capsaicin on feeding behavior and energy intake by adding spicy red pepper to whole meals, and then to appetizers. The results showed that the subjects' appetites decreased both during and after capsaicin-rich meals, and a spicy appetizer beforehand lessened the amount eaten at lunch. This decrease in appetite lead to a subsequent drop in protein and fat intake. In other words: Put a little chile on your food, and you won't eat as much. Try one of the many chile-laced chocolate bars on the market—you'll find that it takes less to satisfy your sweet tooth.

Believe It or Not: Capsaicin Helps Heartburn Victims

A medical experiment at the University of Bologna in Italy has indicated that the active principle in chile peppers may aid sufferers of chronic indigestion. In the study, participants with severe digestive problems without a known cause ingested capsules containing capsaicin, while others took a placebo. Those patients taking capsaicin capsules reported a 60 percent decrease in pain, feelings of fullness, and nausea. Researcher Dr. Mauro Bortolotti suggested that, as with capsaicin used as a topical painkiller, the chemical blocked pain signals going to the brain from the stomach by depleting substance P, a neurotransmitter.

But Does It Give You Softer Hands?
In an experiment on 20 female volunteers, a researcher at the New Mexico Poison Center determined that cooking oil works better than water at easing burns caused by capsaicin. During the study, each volunteer placed both hands in peeled, ground green chile for 40 minutes, then placed one hand in cold water and the other in vegetable oil.

During subsequent interviews, the volunteers indicated that the vegetable oil worked better than water. Perhaps oil works better than water because the capsaicin is oil-soluble but is not miscible in water. Each year the Poison Center receives over 100 calls from women who suffer burns while processing chile for the freezer. Of course, the best way to avoid chile burns is to wear rubber gloves.

Surgeon Lost 70 Pounds On Hot Sauce Diet
Dr. Spiro Antoniades lost 70 pounds and learned to control his appetite on a diet he created after gaining a significant amount of weight doing all the wrong things—overeating, eating too fast, eating the wrong types of foods, doing other things while eating. "I would come home from work and act like a starved maniac. I would eat like crazy. I needed something to push me back, slow down my eating and force me to drink water." The doctor said. His diet answer was hot sauce. "If you have it first, it decreases your appetite and makes you thirsty. So, you drink something and you just calm down for a moment and eat a lot less," he said.

Antonaides said the hot sauce was an effective deterrent for eating behaviors he didn't like, such as eating a log of cheese or wanting to eat a whole chocolate cake. After losing 70 pounds on the diet the doctor decided to write a book about it, called "The Hot Sauce Diet." He says in that one of his favorite tricks is making a "hot sauce bomb" by taking an olive or half a hard-boiled egg with the yolk removed and filling it with hot sauce. He also states that when he's on the diet he puts hot sauce on just about everything–even salad–so he'll eat it slowly. The idea for the idea began while the doctor was still in college. When money was tight, he would put hot sauce on pizza so that he would eat less.

Not everyone agrees that this is a safe or sane way to diet. Health educator and blogger Maddie Ruud challenged whether Dr. Antoniades, an orthopedic surgeon, was qualified to be doling out nutritional advice, and stated that, "Self-deprivation and punishment around food lead to eating disorders and depression, and I don't think Dr. Antoniades is prepared to take responsibility for that." Spoken like a true non-chilehead.

Will Putting Chile Powder in Your Socks Keep Your Feet Warm?

The pro football game between the Denver Broncos and the San Diego Chargers on December 27, 1987, was played in blizzard conditions at Denver Stadium. During a discussion of the bitter cold the players must endure, NBC announcer Jimmy Cefalo discussed a rumor that certain Broncos sprinkled cayenne powder in their socks before the game. According to the story, the cayenne so burned the sweaty feet of the players that they resisted the numbing cold.

I wondered: would it work? After all, similar tales tell of hoboes riding the rails while munching on pickled jalapeños to warm up freezing nights. This hobo legend can be argued, however, because we know that ingesting hot chiles causes gustatory sweating, which cools the body. But since we also know that the topical application of capsaicin can cause severe skin burning—and even blistering in some extreme cases—it makes sense that cayenne could cause a "burning sensation," which might counteract the freezing temperatures.

The major problem with this scenario is that "cold" really means "numb" and "burning sensation" translates as "pain" after a certain point. Although the cayenne might at first give the illusion of heat, it probably would not cause the temperature of the feet to rise significantly, and the resulting pain might be distracting to the player.

It all comes down to this...if time is running out and it's fourth and five to go on your opponent's seven yard line and you're five points behind, would you rather have your feet numb or in agony?

Incidentally, the Broncos won the game but their hot socks were useless in San Diego during the Super Bowl.

A Kneejerk Reaction to Peppers?

In a new twist, the capsaicin that makes so many cry in pain is being used to tame the pain of surgery. Doctors are dripping a highly purified version of capsaicin into open wounds during knee replacement and other highly painful surgeries in an effort to take away some of the initial pain after surgery. The idea is that by overloading the nerves with the hot stuff they will go numb (similar to what happens to your tongue after biting into a habanero). The effects should last for several weeks resulting in fewer narcotics being needed. In a pilot U.S. study of 50 knee replacements, the half treated with capsaicin used less morphine in the 48 hours after surgery and reported less pain for two weeks.

Alternative Medicine Quite Peppery

In a special report in *USA Today* entitled "Can Alternative Medicine Help?", experts Jim Duke, Ph.D. and Deepak Chopra, M.D. were asked about to comment about the effect of alternative medicine on certain ailments. Their comments make them sound like chileheads.

Back Trouble: "Try biting into a hot pepper when the pain is most excruciating. Peppers are almost as inexpensive as aspirin." —Duke

Asthma. "An attack might be alleviated by an early Mexican Maya mixture, hot chocolate with hot pepper." —Duke

Weight Control: "Favor spicy foods with astringent, pungent, and bitter tastes, like bitter greens, horseradish, garlic, fenugreek, curry, onions, and jalapeño peppers, which increase the metabolism." —Chopra

Arthritis: "When pain or stress builds, I have a cup of cayenne-ginger tea. I belive more in hot pepper's ability to densensitize pain and ginger's anti-inflamatory compounds than in anything OK'd by the FDA lately." —Duke

A Person With Ulcers Should Never Eat Chile. Right or wrong?

Investigators at the National University Hospital in Singapore examined the inner lining of the stomach with sophisticated technology to investigate the causes of peptic ulcers.

"A lot of people feel that a pepper is bad for their ulcers and their stomach," said Dr. Jin Y. Kang. "We've shown that it does not harm the stomach and may even help."

The scientists gave patients temporary gut damage with irritants such as aspirin or alcohol, and then applied capsaicin to the damaged areas. Rather than aggravating the damage, capsaicin somehow eased the irritation.

The scientists speculated that that capsaicin stimulates nerve fibers that release a hormone that increases blood flow to the area and helps to protect the stomach from irritants. But they insist that diluted capsaicin—not the peppers themselves—would be the most efficacious.

Why Can Some People Eat Hot Chiles and Others Can't?

The capsaicin receptors and nerve fibers in your mouth are so intertwined that when you eat a hot chile, the chemical pain induced by the capsaicin is perceived as heat by the mouth and brain—and then as pleasure.

Studies by Dr. Barry Green at the Monell Chemical Senses Center in Philadelphia questioned the contention of chile haters that painful foods such as chiles and raw horseradish act as "gustatory sledgehammers, reducing anything in which they are contained to one dimension by overpowering all other tastes." Dr. Green's experiments with such "masking" showed that this belief is not always true. "Some people were able to taste a variety of flavors after eating hot foods," Willoughby wrote, "but others were not."

But why? One theory from cognitive psychology holds that there are two kinds of people: holistic and analytical. When both eat hot and spicy food, the holistic people might believe that the food is too ridiculously hot to taste anything, while the other group "filters the taste through their analytical sensibility and responds, 'Wow, this is great. I can taste all these incredible strong flavors.'" Dr. Green concluded: "The easiest explanation of why people like pain with their food is simply that it adds a whole new dimension to flavor."

The most current research indicates that a lipid molecule called PIP2 plays a crucial role in controlling the strength of the burning sensation caused by capsaicin. A lipid molecule is a fatty molecule, insoluble in water, but soluble in fat solvents and alcohol–just like capsaicin. In the mouth, there is a capsaicin receptor called TRPV1 and the lipid molecule PIP2 is bound to it. In the presence of capsaicin, the PIP2 molecule separates from the receptor, causing a painful sensation.

My Hair is Falling Out! Can Chile Peppers Help?

Once again, capsaicin to the rescue. According to a researcher at Kumamoto University, eating a combo of soybeans and chile peppers is likely to promote hair growth. Assistant professor Kenji Okajima, of the

Graduate School of Medical and Pharmaceutical Sciences, found that combining capsaicin and isoflavone (found in soy beans), helped to restore eyebrow and head hair that had fallen out because of stress. Apparently, capsaicin stimulates the sensory nerves and raises the level of calcitonin gene-related peptide, or CGRP, which in turn raises the level of an "insulinlike growth factor" that is known to be important for hair growth. Isoflavone's job is to promote the production of CGRP. In the case of the first patient, the man's eyebrows and head hair started to grow back after about one month of taking a regimen of chiles and soybeans. "It's difficult to get hair that has fallen out due to stress to grow back," Okajima said. "It's a welcome finding."

More Proof That Your Tummy Can Take The Heat

Legend holds that chile peppers are murder on the human gastro-intestinal system. They are accused of causing heartburn, gastritis, ulcers, and diarrhea among other maladies. Despite such a bad reputation, medical evidence has repeatedly demonstrated that the capsaicin in chile peppers does little or no damage. A recent study at the Veterans Administration Medical Center in Houston backs up the contention that chiles are safe to eat.

The *Journal of the American Medical Association* reported that a team of doctors at the Baylor College of Medicine in Houston conducted a unique experiment utilizing videoendoscopy, the high-tech procedure of inserting a fiber-optic tube and a miniature video camera into the stomach to inspect it visually.

The object of the experiment was to test the generally-held theory that capsaicin, the active

Maybe Dave tried the chile hair loss cure a bit too late.
Photo by Wes Naman

heat chemical in chile peppers, damages the lining of the stomach. The research team, led by Dr. David Graham, subjected 12 volunteers (none were chile lovers) to a series of test meals—bland, plain aspirin, "Mexican," and pizza. After each meal, the endoscope was inserted to determine if "gastric erosions" of the lining had occurred. By far, the most damaging meal was the bland one combined with aspirin.

Not believing their results, the research team then sprayed Tabasco® sauce directly on the stomach lining. There was mucosal damage this time, but it was linked to the vinegar in the sauce. To further test capsaicin alone, the good doctors then injected 30 grams of freshly ground jalapeños directly into the stomach. There was no visible mucosal damage.

Dr. Graham concluded in his study: "We found that ingestion of highly spiced meals by normal individuals did not cause endoscopically demonstrable gastric or duodenal mucosal damage." However, in an interview published in the Los Angeles Times, Dr. Graham admitted that chiles increase gastric acid secretion, but "they add to the flavor and enjoyment of eating and do not appear to cause stomach lining damage."

Salsa Sniffles Snuffed

Medical researchers at the National Institute of Allergy and Infectious Diseases have developed a nasal spray that stops gustatory rhinitis, the dreaded draining of the nasal passages caused by eating hot chiles. Sometimes called the "salsa sniffles," the condition is caused by over-stimulated nerves and is unlike the runniness associated with head colds or allergies, which is triggered by a histamine reaction.

The *Journal of Allergy and Clinical Immunology* described a study where volunteers sprayed an antispasmodic drug up their noses before eating a spicy meal. In 100 percent of the cases, the noses were kept dry, with no adverse side effects. Interesting enough, the drug used was atropine, extracted from the deadly nightshade, *Atropa belladonna*, which belongs to the family *Solanaceae*—as do chile peppers.

Can Pepper Cream Treat Neuralgia?

Barbara Conway of Searchmont, Ontario, was suffering from trigeminal neuralgia, a disease caused by damage to the nerve that brings feeling to the face. The facial pain was so agonizing that she would go to a shopping mall, have an attack, and fall down on the floor screaming in agony.

"Suicide crossed my mind a number of times," she said. "I felt that there would never be a cure, and there was no way that I could go on living like this. But then, out of the blue, we stumbled on the odd, unexpected answer."

That answer to Barbara's agonizing pain was Zostrix, the medicated capsaicin cream used to deaden the pain of shingles. Under a doctor's direction, she began rubbing the cream on her face every time she felt an attack coming on.

"What I know is that when I use Zostrix, I have no facial pain at all," she said. "I'm not afraid to go to the mall anymore."

How Can I Make My Own Capsaicin Cream?

This will make a lotion, but you can make a cream by adding 6 ounces of melted beeswax to the warm, strained oil. Stir thoroughly and shake the bottle until cool.

> 8 to 10 ounces habanero chiles, chopped with the seeds
> 1 quart olive oil

Combine the ingredients and bring to a slow boil. Reduce heat and simmer very gently for 4 hours. Let cool for 4 hours. Repeat this procedure two more times.

Place the mixture in a blender and blend on high for 20 seconds.

Strain the mixture through a sieve that has been lined with muslin (pantyhose will do just as well) and place in small bottles.

Yield: 8 4-ounce containers of lotion or cream.

Variation: You can also enhance the formula by adding 40 drops of lavender oil to the strained lotion.

Caution: Do not rub your eyes after rubbing your skin with this cream!

Pep Up With Peppers

Gram for gram, chile peppers contain more calcium and vitamin A and C than asparagus, celery, and green peas. Also, researchers report that chile pepper consumption seems to rev up metabolism and increase oxidation of fat.

In fact, as a cash crop, peppers are next only to marijuana in per-acre profit...

—chile pepper breeder Dr. Ben Villalon

Chapter 3

Celebrity Chileheads and Best Chile Quotes

You could call me a semi-celebrity, because I'm quite famous in the very narrow niche that is chile peppers and fiery foods. That's not quite enough to place me on the level of Brad Pitt, but there have been occasions when I've been treated like him, especially in Italy, where the newspapers call me *Il Papa del Peperoncini* (guess what that means), and I've been interviewed by the Italian national TV station. I was the guest of honor at the 2010 Peperoncini Festival in Diamante, attended over five days by 150,000 foodies, and I've given a talk, with a translator, at the Accademia Barilla, the famous Italian food history center and library in Parma.

So I'm a little blasé when I meet celebrities and treat them as equals. When I interviewed rocker Alice Cooper back in the seventies, we discussed deep sea fishing. Bobby Flay and I talked about demanding schedules and the necessity to constantly revise "to do" lists over a beer after I appeared on one of his shows. On the *Today Show*, Bryant Gumbel and I discussed, off-camera, his experiences eating peppers while growing up in New Orleans. Mostly—from Paul Prudhomme to Joe Perry, and all the ones mentioned here—they're nice people.

After my appearance on *The Martha Stewart Show* in 2011, all my female friends (okay, some of them) wanted to know what Martha was like. I told them that she was charming, very professional, but a lousy kisser. I don't think they believed me. My most agonizing semi-celebrity experience was on the *Gary Collins Show* when my cooking demonstration had to follow Parents of Murdered Children. Everyone on the set was in tears—the camera operators, the directors, the stage-hands—but not me or Gary. During the break, he apologized to me for having to follow the sob-fest, so I asked him if I should I open my segment with "Enough about murdered children! Let's cook some spicy shrimp!" He replied, "Not enough time, Dave. Your segment's been cut from four minutes to two." But I pulled it off, and when he asked me on-camera what would happen to him if he ate the habanero I gave him, my comeback was: "You would lose your voice, I would have to take over the show, and maybe even get your job." He laughed, and it was genuine.

It's tough work being a semi-celebrity...

The Chilehead Orchestra Leader

According to *The New York Times*, one of the foremost celebrity proponents of chile peppers is Zubin Mehta, music director of New York's Philharmonic Orchestra.

"Oh, God, how I love hot food!" Mehta is quoted as saying by Julie Sahni, writing in the *Times*. "I can't go to American restaurants because I feel like I am in a hospital." To avoid problems like being a guest at a dinner of bland food, Mehta carries chiles with him in tiny, jeweled silver boxes.

A native of India, Mehta's reputation for loving fiery foods is so great that other celebrities joke about it. Comedian Alan King said, "He's the only person I know who puts his own chiles on Mexican food, Indian food, you name it." King also noted: "After dining with him, I don't use a mouthwash, I take Unguentine."

Mehta's favorite chiles are cayenne, tabasco, Scotch bonnet, and "bird" peppers (chiltepins). It figures, as these are some of the hotter more commonly available.

Paul Prudhomme, Scofflaw

If we had hired a sheriff for the Fiery Foods & Barbecue Show back in 1998, he probably would have arrested Paul Prudhomme on a public endangerment charge. I'd known Paul since 1989 when we signed books together at the Fancy Food Show in San Francisco, so it had been easy to persuade him to be our lead Guest Chef at the show. In those days he weighed so much he could hardly walk (he has since lost hundreds of pounds). In fact, we had to use a lift to get him on stage. The crowd for his cooking demo was huge, maybe 800 people. At the end of the demo, he proceeded to serve Cajun food to everyone watching, and I remember thinking, "How did he cook all of that? In the Convention Center kitchen?" Nope. I investigated and found illegal propane tanks and burners at the back of the show hall. I had to laugh because using bottled gas was illegal at the Convention Center, and the Fire Department could have shut the entire show down. But he got away with it and we laughed about it together after the demo.

Julia Child on Palate Death and Other Fairy Tales

On the April 7, 1992 edition of *The CBS News*, noted author and food authority Julia Child made the startling allegation that chile peppers cause "palate death" for those who eat them. Her exact words were:

Interviewer: "Unless, like some, you're afraid that a diet based on salsas and hot peppers will blow your taste buds away for life."

Julia Child: "If one is used to eating that very hot food, I think your palate is mostly gone."

Interviewer: "Just overload, palate overload?"

Julia Child: "I would think so—or, palate death."

Ms. Child offered no evidence to back up her claim and showed a surprising lack of knowledge regarding hot and spicy foods. A quick check of the available literature cited in The Chile Pepper Institute's bibliographies revealed no studies pertaining to chiles interfering with the perception of other tastes such as sweet and sour.

Eating a jalapeño right before tasting angel food cake is not recommended, but there is no evidence that the consumption of hot chiles permanently damages the taste buds. Small amounts of capsaicin produce an effect that fades away within minutes. And, according to University of Colorado neurobiologist John Kinnamon, even after the taste cells have been severely burned by extremely large concentrations of capsaicin, they replace themselves within two weeks. Thus the effects of capsaicin on the palate are temporary, even in extreme situations. We do build up a tolerance to chiles and seem to desire more and more heat, but the phrase "palate death" is an enormous exaggeration.

Bill Wharton—The Boss of Sauce

One morning in the early 70's, the Sauce Boss walked out of his house and found a 1933 vintage National steel guitar in his front yard. Years later he combined his blues with his hot sauce in a big pot of gumbo, made right on stage. Singing the recipe, he mixed music and cooking together into a new medium. So goes the legend of Florida's Bill "Sauce Boss" Wharton, who has fed over 175,000 concert-goers since 1990, cooking gumbo on stage. Jimmy Buffet has sung about him. He's been interviewed on NPR, and CNN, the Food Network and Extra have covered his extravaganzas. Fans all over the country are begging him to "play and a' sway' with the gumbo" at their events, and it's no surprise. Good blues mixed with good hot sauce—can you really go wrong?

The Sauce Boss' magic potion, known as Liquid Summer Hot Sauce, features the Datil chile pepper (a cousin of the Caribbean habanero, but not as hot), plus tomatoes, vinegar, onions, mustard, honey, garlic, olive oil, and salt. It's so good, says the Sauce Boss, "You could marinate your mother-in-law in this stuff!" He also has a Liquid Summer Habanero Hot Sauce, according to his website, "for those who push the envelope of sensation to the threshold of pain; for the endorphin seeker, for the person with a problem." So, whether you're attending one of his concert/gumbo feasts or throwing a blues fest of your own, the Sauce Boss will get you fired up. Think of it as doing the world a favor: "If we could forget our differences for a moment," he says, "sit down to the table, share some dinner, and treat each other like neighbors, maybe we could work some of this stuff out. World politics aside, at least you'll feel better thanks to a full stomach and a hot sauce high."

My favorite memory of Bill is from the final Florida Fiery Foods Show, which had been threatened by Hurricane Irene. Fortunately, the hurricane just brushed Tampa, the show went on as planned, and afterwards our staff repaired to a roadhouse when we had some seafood and liquid refreshments while the Sauce Boss cooked his gumbo on stage. My niece Emily and I waltzed to the hit song of the evening as Bill crooned, "Good night, Irene, good night Irene, I'll see you in my dreams."

Blair on Making Superhot Sauce

Food writer Gwyneth Doland interviewed superhot pioneer Blair Lazar, creator of Blair's Death Sauce:

G. You make all these sauces yourself. Isn't it dangerous to work with super-hot stuff?

B. I have burned myself so many times—and I'm not even saying this in a braggadocious way—that I don't even think about it anymore. It's just something that happens. Seriously. When I'm making a batch, I have to ask other people if the sauce is hot enough. I think I might have burned a few receptors out. I'm a great judge of flavor, but not of heat. The only way I know if it's really, really hot is when my hiccup alarm goes off. I'm not the person to ask, "Is this hot enough?"

G. Because the answer's always no?

B. Right. But again, it's not just about heat. When I attempted to launch my wing sauce, we went through so many rounds of samples and worked on it and worked on it. Everything was great, and we made maybe 500 cases or so. But then I tasted it, and it just wasn't right. I felt like it was lacking the heat; it just wasn't there. We dumped it.

G. You threw it all away? Can't you just add more heat?

B. No. It's not just adding more heat because that changes the flavor profile. You have to start all over again. I'm totally obsessive about it. Really, really obsessive.

G. Do you think you need counseling?

B. Probably. I think if I walked in somewhere and explained how distraught I was over that sauce, I'd be immediately committed.

G. Have you made any particularly memorable mistakes since you've been in the business?

B. You're not writing a book, just an article, right? I don't think you have space for all of my mistakes! But here's one. When I was starting out, I thought that if I just taped all my cases together and put labels on them and sent them off, they'd be fine. I had built up an inventory of something like 25 cases and had made sales to maybe five different places. Nobody told me about packing peanuts or outer carton boxes or anything like that.

G. Uh-oh.

B. There were broken bottles and hot sauce everywhere. I think I annoyed every UPS driver in the country. I had just worked for weeks making the sauce, and it all got wrecked. But I didn't give up! And my customers were great. They knew how hard I'd worked on it, and they forgave me. I still sell to some of them now.

Ted Nugent: Hunter, Gatherer, Griller, Rocker

Food writer Molly Wales interviewed musician and wild game lover Ted Nugent:

Ted Nugent rocks. Ted Nugent hunts. Ted Nugent

Superhot sauce pioneer Blair Lazar, creator of Blair's Death Sauce.

It's Your Chilehead Life

fights relentlessly in support of the Second Amendment. He received praise from former President George Bush for being "a good man" and exemplifying "the founding principles of this great nation." He writes without regard for traditional spelling. He eats squirrel. And he, much to the shock of vegetarians, liberals, animal-rights activists and grocery-store shoppers everywhere, makes an enthusiastic and plausible argument (plausible in that it is entertaining and well thought-out, albeit full of name-calling like "tofu breath") for the supposed ecological, physical and familial benefits of killing your own food and growing your own veggies.

There are many tips, suggestions and recipes in his book *Kill It and Grill It*, for everything from Squirrel Casserole to Bar-B-Que Black Bear, and every one of them proves that Tribe Nugent doesn't just cook— rather, they "dance at the primordial campfire of life." As Ted says, "Everything short of ultimate, ultimately sucks." Whatever that means for you, celebrate life. Rock on.

This shot of Joe Perry was one of our most popular covers of all time for *Fiery Foods & BBQ* Magazine.
Photo by Pat Berrett

Dave DeWitt's Chile Trivia

Aerosmith's Knife-Wielding Chilehead

Editor and creative director Lois Manno recounts this photo shoot with a rock star:

Through a series of amazing connections, lucky breaks, and the help of David Ashley of Ashley Foods, guitar legend Joe Perry agreed to a photo shoot for the cover of *Fiery Foods & BBQ* magazine. He had just launched a new line of hot sauce, Joe Perry's "Rock Your World" Boneyard Brew. I know—it's a long name. But the sauce is righteous.

The shoot was scheduled to happen at an Albuquerque venue right before Aerosmith was due to play a double-bill concert in Albuquerque (with KISS). A meeting room had been set aside, and we were all ready to go with pro photographer Pat Berrett, props, lights, the works. The plan was to shoot Joe holding up a knife, posed to chop fresh veggies on the back of an electric guitar. Clever, huh?

Everything was set up and Joe breezed in looking great in jeans and a bright red shirt. He sat down and we did a couple of test shots, but something wasn't quite right. Putting down the garden-variety butcher knife I'd selected for the shot, Joe said "hey, let's use *my* knife." Reaching into his pocket, he pulled out a huge silver switchblade, flipped up the 6-inch blade, and speared a jalapeño. Everybody went crazy, and we knew we had the money shot. I still have one of the Polaroids from that memorable photo shoot.

Aerosmith's Joe Perry on Hot Sauce

Food writer Molly Wales interviewed Joe after the shoot, and they, of course, discussed hot sauce.

MW: I'm sure you're aware of how many hot sauces are out there. It's incredible.

JP: Yeah. I am a collector, and I do taste a lot of different sauces. I started finding a lot of generic tasting ones, you know. There are a lot of cool labels and lots of cool marketing, but very often what's inside the bottle doesn't live up to the label. And also there was the rage of the extract sauces—I'm a little more organic than that, it was a little bit too much. Every once in a while something will be good, but I don't like a sauce that completely buries the flavor of the food in heat. My kitchen is like most hot sauce people—you've got a variety, but you probably have five to ten of your favorites. And after a while, sorting through that whole wall of sauce, you can kind of tell, "Well I've tasted that one before." But it wasn't about really trying to make something that was so unique, or that was going to all of a sudden blow out the door. I was going to put my name on it because it was something that I liked. And then you take it to the next step and want to share it with people.

Kinky Friedman, the Self-Proclaimed "Salsa Magnate" of Texas

After Kinky Friedman was invited to spend the night at the White House, he emailed President Bush: "I have four women, four editors, and four dogs. Can I bring them all?"

"Just the dogs," replied George W.

What does this have to do with salsa? It's quite a story, so bear with me. First, some background. Richard "Kinky" Friedman is a legend in his own mind, a Texas musician who, with his group the Texas Jewboys, has recorded and performed such songs as "Homo Erectus" and "They Ain't Makin' Jews Like Jesus Anymore." A friend of both Willy Nelson and Laura Bush, Kinky has such a reputation in Texas that he has been able to switch gears from music to the written word. Not only does he have a regular column in *Texas Monthly*, he has written seventeen mystery novels starring himself as an amateur detective–with titles like *Roadkill, Armadillos and Old Lace, The Love Song of J. Edgar Hoover*, and *Elvis, Jesus & Coca Cola*. Former President Bill Clinton is a big fan.

But what does this have to do with salsa? Keep reading, because I asked Kinky the same question. "My new career as a salsa magnate began with a three-legged kitten named Lucky who needed rescuing," he told me. It turns out that Kinky's heart is as soft as his brain, and the saving of Lucky—"she's single pawedly killed two rattlesnakes!," plus 58 dogs, more cats, pigs, donkeys, goats, and turkeys led to the establishment of the Utopia Animal Rescue Ranch near Medina Texas, which is, as Kinky puts it: "a never-kill sanctuary for abused or stray animals, one of whom happens to be me."

Again, what does this have to do with salsa? Okay, okay. The rescue ranch needs funding. Texans love salsa. Kinky admires Paul Newman, so, taking a page from Paul's book, Kinky launched his third career with Kinky Friedman's Private Stock salsas, plus a Kinky Friedman's Kosher Coffee ("imported from Texas") and cigars. "Hot and spicy stuff is good for you," he told me, adding that eating salsa is the only healthy thing he does other than smoke cigars.

Although he claims to have no movie ambitions like Paul Newman had, he admitted to me that Billy Bob Thornton is reading a script of one of his mysteries he would like made into a film.

"And who would play Kinky Friedman in the movie?" I asked him.

"Lionel Richie," he replied.

Chile Plants Flying High

Chilehead Dexter Holland, lead singer of The Offspring, bought a copy of *The Complete Chile Pepper Book* and sent me an email. He wrote, "Got the *Complete Chile Pepper Book* in the mail today...nice one! Looks great, very professional, very informative. I might even try some growing now!" I wrote back and suggested hydroponics under grow lights aboard his private jet!

Celebrities at El Pinto Restaurant

Jim Garcia, my good friend and a spokesperson for New Mexico's largest restaurant—seating more than a thousand people during the summer—likes to keep track of all the celebrities who have eaten there, so he had photos shot during their dining, framed them, and used them to decorate the walls of the lobby and corridors. There are dozens and dozens of them, from rappers I've never heard of to country stars like Clint Black, who gave a private concert there (I sat just six feet from him!). Politicians include both Bush presidents, Barrack Obama, Secretary of State Hillary Clinton, and a bunch of representatives and senators. And I'll bet none of them had to wait for a table!

Best Historical Chile Quotes

The fruit [of the Peruvian Uchu chile] is as indispensable to the natives as salt to the whites.
—Friedrich Alexander von Humboldt,
Political Essays on the Kingdom of New Spain, 1814

Chile, they say, is the king, the soul of the Mexicans—a nutrient, a medicine, a drug, a comfort. For many Mexicans, if it were not for the existence of chile, their national identity would begin to disappear.
—Arturo Lomelli, author of *El Chile y Otros Picantes*

The extravagant use of red pepper among the [New] Mexicans has become truly proverbial. It enters into nearly every dish at every meal, and often so predominates as entirely to conceal the character of the viands.
—Josiah Gregg, *The Commerce of the Prairies*, 1844

The conquest is complete. Hot peppers have taken over the United States.
—Jake Page, writing in *Hippocrates*, 1987

It's Your Chilehead Life

This plant (the Chiltepin), used ceremonially and privately, is thought to drive away approaching sickness. The man who does not eat chile is immediately suspected of being a sorcerer.
—a Tarahumara Indian quoted by Wendell Bennett in his book, *The Tarahumara: An Indian Tribe of Northern Mexico*

The greedy merchants, led by lucre, run,
To the parch'd Indies and the rising sun,
From thence hot pepper and rich drugs they bear,
Bart'ring for spices, their Italian ware.
—Aulus Persius Floccus, Roman satirical poet, A.D. 34-62

Best Contemporary Chile Quotes

Without beets and rhubarb, the food chain would still have ample diversity. Life would go on without turnips. But take away jalapeños and green and red chiles and serrano and habanero peppers and this would be a cold, mean world...
—John Yemma, writing in the *Boston Globe*

A peculiar effect of capsicum is worth mentioning. In Mexico the people are very fond of it; and their bodies get thoroughly saturated with it, and if one of them happens to die on the prairie the vultures will not touch the body on account of its being so impregnated with the capsicum.
—Jethro Kloss, in his bestseller, *Back to Eden*

In the past, chillies were frequently used in the Orient for the purpose of torture, some of the common methods being by introducing them into the nostrils, eyes, vagina or urethra, and burning under the nose...
—R.N. Chopra, author of *Glossary of Indian Medicinal Plants*

Ever notice how pretty the coloring is on a diamondback rattlesnake just before it bites you?
—Patrick Mott of the *Los Angeles Times*

Walk into any major fast food joint or chain restaurant in New Mexico and you will find New
Mexican chiles. Every McDonald's has a double
cheeseburger with green chiles on the menu, and
Pizza Hut has green chiles as a topping In fact,
in all of New Mexico, a pepperoni pizza just isn't
ordered without green chiles, unless it's for a
little kid's birthday party.

> "Gastronaut" Kraig Kraft, writing in
> *Chasing Chiles: Hot Spots Along the Pepper Trail*

What chiles all have in common is a pungency
that is habit-forming and without which food is
insipid and without character...

> —Central American food expert Copeland Marks

He told me to eat hot peppers. He said, "If you
remember to eat hot peppers every day, you'll
never get sick."

> —Musician Marshall Crenshaw, quoted in
> *Rolling Stone* magazine, talking about chilehead Bob Dylan

A single drop of pure capsaicin diluted in 100,000
parts of water will produce a persistent burning
of the tongue. Diluted in one million drops of
water, it still produces a perceptible warmth.

> —*Science News*

It's Your Chilehead Life

America's spiciest spectacle, the National Fiery Foods & BBQ Show, which takes place every March in Albuquerque, New Mexico. This depiction of the crazy show floor was made to celebrate the show's 20th anniversary. Illustration by Lois Manno

Part II

The United States of Spice

Chili concocted outside of Texas is usually a weak, apologetic imitation of the real thing. One of the first things I do when I get home to Texas is have a bowl of red. There is simply nothing better.

—President Lyndon B. Johnson

"Will Howl For Chili." President Lyndon B. Johnson sings with the family dog Yuki while his grandson, Patrick Lyndon Nugent, looks on at the LBJ ranch near Stonewall, Texas. 1968 LBJ Library photo by Yoichi Okamoto

Chapter 4

Contentious
Chili Con Carne

Everything about chili con carne generates some sort of controversy—the spelling of the name, the origin and history of the dish, the proper ingredients for a great recipe, the awesome society and cook-off rivalries, and even what the future holds for the bowl o' red. Arguably, it is the most contentious food in the world, triggering debates as to its origin, authenticity, preparation, and influence on international culinary practices. While researching chili I found a treasure trove of controversial opinions and observations. It is my pleasure to share them with readers with a literary bent–or those who are just bent, period. Perhaps the fiery nature of the dish itself is responsible for such controversy, driving usually rational men and women into frenzies when their conception of the truth is challenged.

I judged many chili cookoffs but the experience—like judging barbecue cookoffs—was not all that challenging or interesting. Cookoff chile, prepared according to CASI or ICS rules, was pretty much the same, with little or no variation, so I disliked the rigidity of the system, and the fact that the organizers often have a very high opinion of not only their cookoff, but of themselves. The director of the International Chili Association was astonished when I told her I would not travel to New Hampshire from Albuquerque to judge, because she wanted me to pay my own way. No, thanks. See how contentious it can get?

So many requests came in for the recipe [referring to her Pedernales River Chili] that it was easier to give the recipe a name, have it printed on a card and make it available. It has been almost as popular as the government pamphlet on the care and feeding of children.

—Lady Bird Johnson

A Chili Prayer Guaranteed to Offend

This prayer was preached by Matthew "Bones" Hooks, a famous African-American range cook, who obviously felt it was a divine calling to cook his favorite food.

"Lord God," he shouted, "you know us old cowhands is forgetful. Sometimes, I can't even recollect what happened yestiday. We is forgetful. We just know daylight from dark, summer, fall, winter, and spring. But I sure hope we don't never forget to thank You before we eat a mess of good chili.

"We don't know why in Your wisdom, You been so doggone good to us. The heathen Chinee don't have no chili ever. The Frenchmens is left out. The Rooshians don't know no more about chili than a hog knows about a side saddle. Even the Meskins don't get a good whiff of it unless they stay around here.

"Chili eaters is some of Your chosen people. We don't know why You been so doggone good to us. But Lord, God, don't never think that we ain't grateful for this chili we about to eat. Amen."

"Mess Scene on Roundup" circa 1887. What do you bet they were eating chile con carne?
John C. H. Grabill Collection, Library of Congress

Dave DeWitt's Chile Trivia

What, Exactly, IS Chili?

The "basics" are to chili-making what the scales
are to music. Once known, the various culinary
tunes that can be played are endless.

—Johnearl Rae and James McCormick,
authors of *The Chili Cookbook*

Chili—real chili—chili Texas-style, must have the
strength to chin itself, even with a big rock in
the bottom of the pot. It is an all-purpose invigo-
rator, a reliable antibiotic for melancholy, and a
prime mover when one's world seems to stand on
dead center. It is a panacea to man in want or
woe.

—Joe E. Cooper, author of *With or Without Beans*

I have a theory that real chili is such a basic,
functional dish that anyone can make it from
the basic ingredients—rough meat, chile peppers,
and a few common spices available to hungry
individuals—and they'll eventually come up with
pretty much the same kind of recipe that was
for most of a century a staple of Texas tables. So
all we have to do to get back to real chili is to
get rid of the elitist nonsense.

—Sam Pendergrast, author of *Zen Chili*

Chili, chili con carne, Texas red—whatever you
call that savory concoction of meat, grease, and
fire—is the natural child of the arguing state of
mind. There's no recipe for it, only disputation,
and almost anyone's first thought after a taste of
somebody else's version, no matter how much it
pleasures the throat, is that they could make it
better.

—John Thorne, author of *Just Another Bowl of Texas Red*

Favorite Names for Competition Chili Teams

Armadillo Express, Medic Alert, Tail End of Texas, Snake Pit Chili, Dead
Serious, Hot Rod, Beer Hawgs, I'm Too Sexy for This, Heartburn Helper,
Lonestar Roughnecks, The Partial Texans, Law West of the Pecos, Hose

Heads, Shady Bunch, Pharter Starters, Chili Willy, Red Hot Chili Preppers, Roadkill Caterers, Blow Your Butt Off Chili, We're Just Here for the Beer, Harry Pooter and the Wizards of Hogfart

Favorite Names for Weirdo Chilis

Blazing Saddles Chili, Dragon Fire Chili, Boiled Cigar Butts and Sheep Dip Chili, Triple XXX Chili, Brother Willy & Sister Lilly's Traveling Salvation Army Chili, Voodoo Chili, Chicken Lips Chili, Warlock Chili, Happy Heine Chili, Brimstone Broth, Hillbilly Chili, Scorpion Breath Chili, Wildfire Chili, Capital Punishment Chili, Terk's Tekil-Ya Chili, Vampire Chili, Buffalo Butt Chili, Werewolf Chili, Pineal Nectar Chili, Mephistophelean Chili, Satan's Soup Chili, Ragin' Cajun Chili, Bubba's Big Bang Recycled Chili.

A Brief History of Canned Chili

According to Wikipedia, Willie Gebhardt, originally of New Braunfels, Texas, and later of San Antonio, produced the first canned chili in 1908. Rancher Lyman Davis near Corsicana, Texas, developed Wolf Brand Chili in 1885. He owned a meat market and was a particular fan of Texas-style chili. In the 1880s, in partnership with an experienced range cook, he began producing heavily spiced chili based on chunks of lean beef and rendered beef suet, which he sold by the pot to local cafés. In 1921, Davis began canning his product, naming it for his pet wolf "Kaiser Bill." Wolf Brand canned chili was a favorite of Will Rogers, who always took along a case when traveling and performing in other regions of the world. Ernest Tubb, the country singer, was such a fan that one Texas hotel maintained a supply of Wolf Brand for his visits. Both the Gebhardt and Wolf brands are now owned by ConAgra Foods, Inc. In the UK, the most popular brand of canned chili is sold by Stagg, a division of Hormel foods.

Where Did Chili Cook-offs Begin?

The first chili cook-off known to modern man took place in 1967 in the south Texas ghost town of Terlingua (once a thriving mercury-mining town of 5,000 people). It was a two-man cook-off between Texas chili champ Wick Fowler (a Dallas and Denton newspaper reporter) and humorist/author H. Allen Smith, which ended in a tie.

The cook-off challenge started when H. Allen Smith wrote a story for the *Holiday* magazine entitled *Nobody Knows More About Chili Than I Do*. The cook-off competition ended in a tie vote when the tie-breaker judge allowed someone to ram a spoonful of chili into his mouth and he promptly spit it all over the referee's foot and then went into convulsions. He rammed a handkerchief down his throat and pronounced himself unable to go on. He then declared a one-year moratorium on the World Championship Chili Cook-off.

Smith had this to say about Texas chili: "There are fiends incarnate, mostly Texans, who put chopped celery in their chili, and the Dallas journalist, Frank X. Tolbert, who has been touted as the Glorious State's leading authority on chili, throws in corn meal. Heaven help us one and all! You might as well throw in some puffed rice, or a handful of shredded alfalfa, or a few Maraschino cherries."

The Chilosophers Speak: Proverbs

Any man smart enough to steal a horse can whip up a passable batch of chili.

—Anonymous

Terlingua, Texas is generally accepted as the birthplace of the chili cookoff. The first Terlingua Chili Championship took place in 1967, and is still going strong. This image is from the 2010 event poster created by tattoo artist Adam Hays.

The United States of Spice

Chili is a stew that can sit on a cold stove and boil gently.

—Wally Boren

Good chili is harder than the Devil to find and almost as rare in restaurants as Braised Unicorn.

—Floyd and Bessie Cogan

Good chili must not perish from the earth.

—Joe E. Cooper

Chili should have the warmth of a New Mexico sunset and the bravado of a Texas stampede.

—David Schwadron

One man's chili is another man's axle grease. If a guy wants to toss in an armadillo, I don't argue with him—I just don't eat with him.

—Carroll Shelby, co-founder
of CASI (Chili Appreciation Society International)

I judge a town by its chili.

—Will Rogers

Chili Goes to the Dogs

From chili cook John "Professor Fosdick" Foster comes this true story: "From the start we have had a tradition of making up humorous labels for our team and putting them on soup cans for display purposes, or selling them for $1.00 each to raise money for the charity at hand. We would always tell the people that it was only soup that was in the can itself. We found that on more than one occasion, people would steal our cans, probably assuming our chili was inside. So, we started putting our labels on cans of dog food. Hopefully, those that tried to circumvent the charity donation got an unpleasant surprise."

The First Ladies of Chili

Because H. Allen Smith believed that "no one should be permitted to cook chili while then and there being a female person," women under the age of 90 were banned from most early chili cook-offs. But chili changed with the times when Allegani Jani Schofield and some friends created the Hell Hath No Fury Chili Society and held the women-only

Susan B. Anthony Memorial Cook-In in Luckenbach. Allegani Jani went on to win at Terlingua in 1974 with her famous Hot Pants Chili.

Is This Your Chili on Drugs?
We'd like to know what food writers Jane and Michael Stern were smoking when they wrote this about chili con carne: "A true Texas bowl of red is a stunning vision, reminiscent of a Technicolor sunset created in a Hollywood studio: opaque currents of molten mahogany, lustrous orange, and cordovan are flecked with grains of spice and swirled with rivulets of limpid grease."

Chili...With Beans or Without?
The debate continues to rage about whether or not chili con carne should contain beans. Generally, true chili *aficionados* would never allow a bean to find its way into the chili pot. However, commercial canned chili can be found with or without beans, so somebody somewhere must prefer beans in their bowl.

According to *Consumer Reports*, the answer to this question depends on your geography: "In some areas it's kidney beans. In other areas it's pinto beans. In some areas it's no beans. In Ohio some people pour chili over spaghetti. In other places this could get you shot. This applies to the heat, too. The farther South you go, the hotter it gets. Not surprisingly, around New Orleans, using Tabasco® Sauce for the heat is not only accepted but expected. Like barbecue, this question deals with the status of chili con carne as a religion rather than as a food."

What's Cincinnati Chili and How is it Different?
It's about as different from Texas chili con carne as you can get. This Ohio version of chili seems to have originated with immigrant food vendors who modified a traditional Macedonian stew and served it over spaghetti. Tom and John Kiradjieff began serving the chili in 1922 at their hot dog stand, and then opened the first chili parlor, called The Empress.

Cincinnati chili contains some ingredients you'd never find in a Texas bowl o' red, including cinnamon, cloves, allspice, or chocolate. In contrast to the robust, chunky texture of Texas chili, Cincinnati's version is thinner, more like a sauce. It's often served over spaghetti or hot dogs and topped with cheese, onions, and beans. A lot of Texans are retching right about now as they read this.

I could have been a typical rich man's brat and ridden fast women and walked with slow horses, and the company never would have made it. But I've given my time and my energies, such as I have been able to develop, to Tabasco®, and I've earned my position here.

—Walter S. McIlhenny, circa 1974

Walter's son Paul McIlhenny shows Dave some pepper mash at the plant on Avery Island, Louisiana in 1994. Photo by Patrick Holian

Dave DeWitt's Chile Trivia

Chapter 5

Strange Brew: Salsas & Hot Sauces from All Over

What is this stuff, anyway?

"One man's hot sauce is another man's salsa," says food writer Kim Pierce, and I couldn't agree more. Beyond the need for definitions, there are so many different recipe variations on the concept of hot sauce that they boggle the mind.

"One difficulty in discussing hot sauces is that the word 'sauce' is not aways used in a precise manner," observes food writer Tom Hudgins. "Sometimes the word is used to mean a liquid sauce that is preserved by bottling or canning—such as the fish sauces of the Orient or such popular modern preparations as Worcestershire sauce. Sometimes 'sauce' is used to designate a thicker vegetable sauce that is cooked and then puréed. And sometimes the word is used to designate a fresh or cooked condiment that is closer to a relish."

Why are North Americans consuming record amounts of hot sauce these days? "Hot sauces are guilt-free attitude adjustors for the prudent Nineties," says food writer Alison Cook. "They're cheap. They're legal. Best of all, they take your body on a wild metabolic ride that offers the illusion of danger, then leaves you flooded with mood-enhancing endorphins. And did I mention that hot sauces are packed with vitamins, are low in fat, and possess an almost magical power to transform that which is dull (read: fatless and saltless food) into that which is interesting?" Joe Cahn, owner of the New Orleans School of

Cooking, has another reason. "Hot sauce is like wine," he says. "There's one for each type of food."

My worst experience with hot sauce was at one of the first Austin Hot Sauce festivals, when I was judging them. It was 99 degrees in the shade with the humidity at 99 percent and I was seated in front of a large speaker blaring out conjunto music. I had to taste and rate 200 sauces—most of them made by amateurs. After I threatened never to judge again, the organizers moved the next year's judging indoors, in air conditioning, and provided all the beer we wanted. That was much better. My best hot sauce experience was writing *The Hot Sauce Bible* (1996) with Chuck Evans. That was a lot of fun!

I firmly believe that the trend toward hot sauces and other fiery foods represents a paradigm shift in the eating habits of North Americans. And that trend is here to stay—and will certainly grow. When was the last time you heard someone say: "Oh, I used to eat hot and spicy, but now I'm back to bland?"

One of the more curious uses of Louisiana-style hot sauce is to pour some of it into a plastic or cellophane bag of fried pork rinds, hold the bag closed, and gently shake it a few times. This makes the relatively bland pork rinds much tastier.

—Food writer Tom Hudgins

Europe likes salsa. In Germany and England, they learned to eat more of the Southwest or Old El Paso types. But these salsas are not really authentic. The closer you get to the Spanish-speaking population, the more exposure there is to the authentic flavors.

—Ignacio "Nacho" Hernandez,
president of online Mexican food megasite MexGrocer.com

Industrial espionage is common in the picante sauce business. In fact, strangers have been found lurking around dumpsters at Pace's San Antonio plant, trying to discover what kind of tomato paste the company uses.

—Food writer Hilary Hylton

Although the U. S. now consumes more salsa than ketchup, ancestral memories of indigenous flavors and methods of food preparation have little to do with the popularity of salsa in the North. Even in the American Southwest—with its common border with Mexico—the consumption of salsa often has less to do with cultural origins than with cultural fusion.

—Business writer Randall Frost

Compound in Salsa May Fight Food Poisoning

According to the American Chemical Society, researches have found a compound in cilantro—a key ingredient in many salsas—that kills harmful *Salmonella* bacteria. The compound, dodecenal, also shows promise as a natural and safe food additive that might help prevent food-borne illnesses. Researches claim that dodecenal, which is found in both the leaves and the seeds of cilantro, is the only naturally oc-curring antibacterial that is more effective than gentamicin, the com-monly used medicinal antibiotic. Says study leader Isao Kubo, Ph.D., "The study suggests that people should eat more salsa with their food, especially fresh salsa." Pass the chips!

Does Salsa Really Outsell Ketchup?

As with most statistics, it depends on how you spin the data. For in-stance, if you're looking at total volume sold, ketchup is the champ. But if the count is based on the amount spent overall, salsa takes the lead. It's important to remember, however, that salsa costs more per ounce than ketchup. In 2002 Hispanic births in this country outpaced Anglo births for the first time. Undoubtedly, this Latino population expansion translates into a buying public more attuned culturally to using products that contain chiles. So the answer is yes, but no.

Further Dissing of Ketchup

"Ketchup, long the king of American condiments, has been dethroned. Industry analysts were quick to confirm that salsa's ascendency was not the work of fringe or elitist groups with abberant appetites. 'The taste for salsa is as mainstream as apple pie,' said David A. Weiss, the president of Packaged Facts, Inc., a market research firm in New York. Epicures and food historians view the toppling of ketchup as the manifest destiny of good taste. Ketchup, that sugar-sweetened complement to fried food and meat, symbolizes 'the bland old British-based American diet,' said Elizabeth Rozin, a specialist in ethnic foods. It's still good on fries.

Pro-Ketchup Political Wrangling
Former U.S. Representative Robert Underwood (D-Guam) wrote his colleagues in the House the following satirical piece in reaction to proposed "English-Only" legislation: "I was surprised to learn that salsa has replaced ketchup as our nation's leading condiment. I'm preparing to draft 'Ketchup-only' legislation to make the use of ketchup mandatory in all government food services. Our nation was founded on commonality. Salsa, and to a great extent, soy sauce, threaten the dietary fiber of our nation. If people come to this country, they should be prepared to use our condiments. Thank you for supporting Ketchup-only. Underwood would probably be further surprised to learn that ketchup originated in Indonesia and that hot and spicy ketchups in this country date back to Campbell's Tabasco® Ketchup in 1911.

The Legend of Arthur "Popie" Devillier
Born in Southern Louisiana in the "Bayou Country," Arthur Devillier left home at the ripe old age of thirteen, settling into work as a lumberjack in one of the area logging camps. According to his late great grandson, Kent Cashio, Arthur "Popie" Devillier (*Popie* was a name usually given to a Cajun grandfather by his grandson), became a cook for a lumber camp, and was taught the ropes by a French cook and a Choctaw Indian assistant. In 1893 it is said that Popie Devillier developed his legendary hot sauce "HOTTER'n HELL."

Relying on his Choctaw/ Cajun heritage, he created the sauce by  blending eight spices, including cloves, which many of the workers used to place in their mouths after a meal to ease the burn and soothe the tongue. He then slow-cooked the sauce to yield a spicy hot, yet full flavored hot sauce. The HOTTER'n HELL recipe was passed down the family tree for more than 90 years until 1992 when Kent, seeing the potential in the market for a recipe that had endeared it-self to the lumberjacks and families of the French-owned Louisiana Territory, introduced the product to the public as POPIE'S HOTTER'n HELL SAUCE. Doug Cashio, great-great grandson of the legendary Popie DeVillier, has reclaimed his family heritage and relaunched the "Hotter'n Hell" hot sauce originated by his great-great grandfather in 1893. Popie's sauce may now be made in Pensacola Florida, but its heart is still deep in the Louisiana bayou, as demonstrated by its mas-cot—the alligator—and a tagline that says, "Shake the Devil Out of It!"

What's the Difference Between Hot Sauce and Salsa?

Salsas and sauces are essential to Southwestern cuisine. They are sim-ilar in that they utilize chile peppers of one variety or another, and contain fresh vegetables commonly grown in the Southwestern states. The difference between them is simple—salsas are usually uncooked, and sauces are usually cooked." This applies north of the border, but in Mexico, all sauces are referred to as "salsas.

Oldest Tabasco® Bottle Found

A 135-year-old Tabasco® bottle was recovered and reconstructed from 21 glass fragments found in an archaeological site of the historic Bos-ton Saloon in Virginia City, Nevada. Ashley Dumas, a graduate student at the University of Alabama who directed the excavations at the origi-nal Tabasco® factory, said that the bottle found in the Comstock min-ing district of Virginia City is a Type 1a bottle, one of the earliest forms known. Edmund McIlhenny began bottling Tabasco® in 1868, and the Boston Saloon operated between 1864 and 1875.

Hot Sauce Detoxifies Raw Oysters

If you've ever suffered food poisoning from tainted raw oysters, as I have (it was an horrendous experience), read on. A team of scientists from the Louisiana State University Medical Center has performed a series of tests on a bacterium, *Vibrio vulnificus*, found in some raw oys-ters, which causes symptoms ranging from mild diarrhea to danger-ous blood poisoning. Some of the suggested oyster treatments ranged from adjusting the storage temperature downward, to heat-shocking them, to zapping them with radiation.

Enter hot sauce. The LSU scientists recounted their experiments with test tubes full of oyster bacteria. Ketchup added to the test tubes had little effect. Lemon juice worked "moderately well," as did horse-radish. But straight hot sauce from a bottle killed all bacteria in one minute flat. Even diluted sixteen to one, the hot sauce killed all the bacteria in five minutes.

"Some of the findings were a little astonishing to us," said Dr. Kenneth Aldridge, one of the researchers. "We had no idea these condiments would be so powerful." They also tested three other varieties of *Vibrio* bacteria, as well as *E. coli*, *Shigella*, and *Salmonella*. Hot sauce killed them all.

If seafood lovers ever needed a reason for using hot sauce, they have it now. Is this the future for sushi and sashimi?

Pace Picante Product of Pro Shop?
"People ask me how I came across my recipe for picante sauce," said Pace Foods founder David Pace, "and I say, 'By trial and error.' But my friends will tell you that's a big lie, that the golfers at the neighborhood golf shop came up with the recipe. They were my guinea pigs."

Tastier Chips & Salsa Through Chemistry
Scientists at the Agricultural Research Service in Albany, California isolated the key ingredient in the unique aroma and flavor of yellow corn tortillas, and it is a natural compound called 2-aminoacetophenone. Researchers Ronald Buttery and Louisa Ling purchased a wide range of corn tortilla products at a local supermarket and then subjected them to a gas chromatograph and a mass spectrometer. They isolated about thirty key flavor elements and then used a group of twenty people who used their noses to select the one element most crucial to aroma and flavor in corn products. The winner was 2-aminoacetophenone, and it could be used to improve the flavor of many brands of tortilla chips on the market. About $2.5 billion worth of tortilla chips are sold annually, and sales have topped microwave popcorn and are closing fast on potato chip. The average American spends about $10 per year on tortilla chips. The average chilehead probably spends ten times that amount to feed the salsa habit.

What's Really the Best Way to Cool a Hot Sauce Burn?
Along the gustatory highway, you will at some point overdo the hot sauce, and chile peppers will do the Flamenco in your mouth. What do you do? As we all know, the cause of that incredible burning sensation is the oil that the chile pod produces called capsaicin. The most common remedies in cooling the fire are a swig of water or a gulp of beer. Alas, as liquid and oil do not mix, this only provides temporary relief.

Soft drinks are a little better as the sugar cuts the heat, yet this is also temporary. Better yet, milk or ice cream or yogurt provide a soothing coating and relief tends to come faster with dairy products.

Supposedly tortillas, bread, and other starches such as rice and potatoes provide relief, as they help sop up the liquid heat, but I have found these cures to be ineffective as well. For a dessert cool-down, try chocolate. The creaminess (from the cocoa butter) coats the mouth, while the sugars and flavor fight the chile oil and seem to neutralize the heat. And what a perfect way to finish off a great meal.

Monk Sauce Will Bring You to Your Knees

The Benedictine monks at the Subiaco Abbey in Arkansas River Valley have a rather unexpected hobby…they make hot sauce. It all started when Father Richard Walz was stationed in Belize to start a new monastery. While there he learned to grow habanero peppers, and came up with a recipe for hot sauce. They used the sauce at their retreat center, and it gained such popularity that, Father Walz says, "We sort of fell into the idea of producing it," and they started selling the sauces in Belize.

Upon his return to Subiaco Abbey, he brought habanero seeds from Belize. They planted the first crop in the summer of 2003 and made more than 100 gallons of hot sauce, which they gave away or sold in 8-ounce bottles. There are two sauces (red and green), which Father Walz describes as, "very hot. There are a lot of habaneros in the sauces—in fact they're primarily habaneros. We've had a lot of assurances that this is a HOT hot sauce." Amen to that!

The United States of Spice

Trappey's Gives Tabasco® the "Screw You" Treatment

Journalist Doug Cress described this early hot sauce rivalry: "In the early days of Southern pepper lore, the Tabasco® war raged across southern Louisiana and eventually found its way to the United States Supreme Court. The McIlhenny Company which began producing its famous Tabasco® sauce in Avery Island, Louisiana, in 1868, spent the next fifty years defending its sole right to the the the name "Tabasco" in court, and the losers took it hard. The former president of arch-rival Trappey's Pepper Sauce, a large, muscular man given to grudges, habitually screwed the cap on every bottle of McIlhenny's sauce supertight whenever he encountered one in a restaurant. Frustrated, diners would invariably reach for the only other option: Trappey's."

Jailhouse Fire: Hot Sauce Created With Conviction

Inmates at a Florida jail have been growing hot peppers as part of a horticulture program at the jail, and one of them made a suggestion to make the peppers into a hot sauce.

Allen Boatman, the horticulture program's director, agreed it would be a good idea, and residents of the Falkenburg Road Jail in Brandon are now the proud makers of Jailhouse Fire hot sauce.

"The food here is kind of institutionalized, so it helps," Boatman said.

In one of the most innovative ad campaigns around, Jailhouse Fire's series of posters promoted the tougher aspects of a hot sauce made by jailbirds: "It's so lethal" and "Murder on your taste buds" are two of the featured taglines.

Dave DeWitt's Chile Trivia

There are three flavors of Jailhouse Fire: Original, Smoke, and No Escape. The revenue goes back to the inmate canteen fund and to culinary and horticulture programs for inmates.

The sauce is made from a mixture of several varieties of herbs and hot peppers, all grown on more than 6 acres behind the jail. Among the peppers are habaneros, scotch bonnets and jalapeños.

"It's a macho thing," Boatman said. "You know, 'I can eat the hottest pepper.'"

Confessions of a Pepper Sauce Smuggler

Thanks to Robb Walsh from Texas, the Indiana Jones of Food Writers, for sharing this story of chilehead high adventure on the border:

"Just show me the pills and everything will be fine," the Customs agent repeated for the third time.

"But I don't have any pills," I continued to insist.

Maybe it was my appearance that convinced the Customs Agent at the U.S. border I was smuggling something. My long hair was matted and my clothes looked slept in. My eyes were glassy and I hadn't shaved lately. I had boarded the night train after midnight in San Luis Potosi, drank Tequila until the wee hours with some Mexicans I had just met, and slept poorly in the Pullman bunk. I woke up as we pulled into Nuevo Laredo looking less than stylish in my dirty, Tequila-scented clothes of the day before.

"So what's in these bottles?" the Customs Agent asked, pulling dozens of containers wrapped in brown paper out of my bag. His grin disappeared when he discovered that each package contained a carefully wrapped bottle of pepper sauce.

"I collect hot sauce," I said as matter-of-factly as possible.

He looked at me with the disbelief customs agents reserve for obvious smugglers, as if collecting hot sauce were somehow peculiar.

"All of these bottles contain hot sauce?" he asked, checking one more time to see if I wanted to change my story.

"Yes sir, hot sauce in every one," I answered. He held one up to the light and shook it to see if there were pills or marijuana seeds floating around inside.

"What in God's name do you do with all this hot sauce?" he wanted to know.

While smart alecky answers flooded my brain, I resisted the temptation to antagonize this man. One wrong move and he would start dumping out my hot sauces and then where would I be?

"I put it on my food," I deadpanned.

"Well, you must like it awful hot," he said as he waved me on, back into the bosom of my own country.

Salsa: It's Not Just for Breakfast Anymore

Are you still using salsa as a dip for chips? That's so yesterday. With the myriad of salsa combinations and flavors—both bottled and freshly prepared—there are many more dimensions to this simple and spicy condiment. As a marinade and baste, it's great for preparing just about anything you can put on the grill. As a topping, think grilled meats, baked potatoes, and even pizzas. As an ingredient, imagine adding it to your meatloaf, scrambled eggs, or chili con queso. As a filling, try it with won tons, empanadas, or egg rolls. Here are some additional ideas for adding salsas to your summer meals.

Beverages. Salsa in a bloody mary or virgin mary? Simply use your blender. Instead of buying a chile pepper vodka, add salsa to your favorite vodka, let it steep for a few days, strain it though cheesecloth and *voila*, salsa-infused vodka to astonish your friends.

Breakfast. Picture your favorite breakfast burrito transformed by your favorite salsa. Or huevos rancheros. Even menudo, the real breakfast of champions, needs salsa in it. And yes, you can make breakfast sausage with salsa in it. My wife regularly makes our Sunday breakfast omelets with salsa and some interesting cheese, like feta or gorgonzola.

Appetizers. Add salsas to commercial dips for an instant flavor improvement. Shrimp cocktails with salsa replacing the standard cocktail sauce? Works for me. Want to shock your guests? Make a pâté the standard way but add salsa to it. For toast points, such an old-school app can be updated with a cheddar-salsa spread.

Seafood. Take a whole, cleaned fish in a Pyrex glass bowl, pour your favorite salsa over it, and bake it with indirect heat in a closed grill outside. Add salsa to Shrimp Creole, tuna salad, fish chowder, ceviche, raw oysters and clams, or top sashimi with it like we were served in Todos Santos, Baja California Sur.

Meat. Slice open the thickest pork chop you can find and stuff it with salsa before grilling. Add salsa to any meat gravies you are making. When basting barbecue, but sure your BBQ sauce has some salsa mixed into it. Add it to your chili con carne, mix it in with your ground beef for hamburgers or chorizo. Making carnitas? Use salsa during the last minute of frying them.

Poultry. For Thanksgiving, surprise the family with cornbread-salsa stuffing in the turkey. Chicken pot pie with chipotle salsa in it? Fantastic. Take a hint from the cooks in Barbados: lift the chicken skin from the meat and insert salsa (they use a spicy herb blend) before frying, roasting, or grilling. Chicken soup for the salsa soul? I love it. Can you imagine chopped liver with salsa? I can, on dark rye.

Side Dishes. Baked beans will never be the same after you've cooked them with salsa. When preparing rice pilaf, substitute 1/4 cup of salsa for 1/4 cup of the stock, and wow! Calabacitas with salsa is a Southwest treat, as are salsa-filled, fried squash blossoms. Instead of garlic mashed potatoes, use salsa, which also gives them some color. And of course, salsa makes a great tomato salad dressing. Salsa-scalloped potatoes are a real treat. If you live in the South, think about salsa and grits.

Baked Goods. Here's the general rule of thumb when baking with something like salsa: use it as part of the liquid measurement in the recipe. Then, if the batter looks too dry, add more liquid, a little at a time. You could even use the juice from the salsa. Start with something simple-like cornbread. It's sometimes a hit or a miss in baking; just keep experimenting and keep notes.

Desserts. It's sweet heat time, with fruit salsa over vanilla ice cream. Mix some mango salsa into your fruit pie filling. Instead of bananas foster, why not bananas sweet salsa? And with some red chile salsa, you can easily make a warm chocolate pie or custard.

Warning: After you've tried all these ideas, you may become a salsaholic. Lucky you.

What Does Salsa Have to do with Dancing?

There's an interesting connection between them. According to the website Salsa-Dancing Addict.com, Salsa music originated in Cuba and is a mixture of many dance styles from Latin American countries, blended with African rhythms and French country dances. This exuberant art form was carried to Mexico City and New York around the time of World War II.

The word "Salsa" was first applied to danceable Latin music in 1933, when Cuban composer Ignacio Piñero wrote the song Échale Salsita. Apparently he was inspired to apply the spicy moniker after consuming some particularly bland New York cuisine (lox & bagel, anyone?). In the 1960s Salsa music became commercially popular. One of the early Salsa albums was the Cal Tjader Quintet plus 5's lush creation *Soul Sauce/Cal Tjader*, the cover of which featured a fork on a plate of red beans and chile alongside an opened bottle of Tabasco® sauce.

Chile is not going to come and go, like kiwi fruit. It's going to stay, like rock 'n' roll.

—Dr. Paul Bosland, aka "Mr. Chileman,"Director of
New Mexico State University's
Chile Pepper Institute

In 2006, Dr. Paul Bosland and the New Mexico State University's Chile Pepper Institute won a Guinness World Record for discovering the world's hottest chile pepper, the 'Bhut Jolokia'. Ironically, Bosland also developed a heatless jalapeño and 'NuMex Suave', a mild habanero.

Chapter 6

Chile Growing Pains and Gains

My parents were avid gardeners in the '50s, with my mother entering her tulips in flower shows and my father a dedicated tomato grower. My brother Rick and I were the grunts, the ones who turned the compost and mixed the potting soil according to Dad's formula of aged compost, peat moss, sand, and topsoil. But we really learned how to grow things, an obsession we both still fortunately possess.

I couldn't have a garden in college and graduate school, because of the apartments and small houses I first inhabited in Richmond, Virginia. But then I moved to a much larger house and started gardening again, and have had a garden every year since, about forty of them. I started growing chiles in 1975, the first season after I moved to Albuquerque, and have had a crop every year.

Dr. Paul Bosland, the famous chile breeder at New Mexico State University, and I have written three chile pepper gardening books together, and that meant a lot of field work and experimentation—even more fun, and for a while Paul held the Guinness World Record for hottest chile grown, the 'Bhut Jolokia' at slightly over one million Scoville Heat Units. And that brings up the biggest current subject, superhot chiles. More about those in chapter 14.

Now I have a financial interest in some superhot chile fields in Las Cruces, my first foray into farming, which is defined as gardening taken to a larger scale while hoping to make a profit. With tractors. Wish me luck.

When them chile pods ripen
You gotta pick 'em before they swipe 'em
In them ole chile fields back home.
> —Hank and Louie Wickham, New Mexico Troubadours

Why No Smoking in the Chile Field?

Q. Smoking cigarettes in chile fields is often prohibited because:
- (a) the smoke causes the peppers' stomata to close, inhibiting osmosis;
- (b) used cigarette ends ("butts") can pollute the soil;
- (c) an insidious disease known as tobacco mosaic virus may be transmitted;
- (d) pepper pickers are susceptible to tobacco smoke and high temperatures in the field during summer harvest, causing them to faint.

A. (c) Tobacco and chiles are both members of *Solanaceae*, the Nightshade family. Viruses may be transmitted between various species of this family.

The Top 10 Greatest Myths About Chile Growing

By Cap Farmer, a former marijuana grower who has switched to chiles to prevent his house and property from being seized by the Feds.

1. You Can Plan on a Great Garden This Year!

Guest horticulturist Cap Farmer shares his dopey insights into chile gardening.

The Myth: You've read all the books, blogs, and sites about chile gardening and you know this year you'll have a record chile pod yield.

The Truth: Dude, it's not that easy. There are dark forces at work far beyond your control, like when my brother Rick's chile field was totally trashed by five inches of rain in two hours. Another time, my own beloved home garden was wiped out by superfreak 70 mph winds. Talk about a blow job! Then there's hail, tornados, early frost, curly top virus, root rot, marauding rabbits, DEA agents

dressed up like snails, slugs, hornworms, thrips, and even chile thieves.
What you need most is luck!

2. Fertilize for More Pods!
The Myth: Since corn grows better when you add lots of nitrogen, so will chiles.

The Truth: Do you have recipes for lots of chile pepper leaves? Have you figured out how to smoke them for a pleasant, reality-altering buzz? Because that's what you'll get with a lot of nitrogen: leaves and no pods…which is sort of like stems but no buds. Use only aged compost as a fertilizer. Old shit is still good shit, as they say.

3. Cure Chile Plant Diseases Instantly!
The Myth: Using simple organic gardening techniques will prevent or cure most chile pepper diseases.

The Truth: I remember the time my friend and I both had colds and we tried to cure ourselves in a Jamaican Steam Bath. That worked about as well as organic disease-control. Most of the crappy stuff that makes your chile plants sick is transmitted by vectors like white fly and leafhoppers that are seriously gnarly. And once your plants get a viral disease like curly top, they are doomed to die. You wouldn't think that something with such a cute name could kill your plants, but there you are.

4. Fun in the Full Sun—All Day Long!
The Myth: All chiles grow best in full sun.

The Truth: Just like albino redheads, right? Some chiles do grow best in full sun, but it all depends on latitude and altitude. The further north you live, and at lower altitudes, full sun is fine. Now, I'm usu-

The United States of Spice

ally all for being as high as possible. But if you go south and higher in elevation, full sun with all its ultraviolet light can burn the crap out of your plants, causing sunscald on the pods and leaf drop on more sensitive varieties like habaneros, which need some shading. And if you've ever sunburned your pod, dude, you know it's a mistake you only make once.

5. Trim the Flowers and Produce More Pods!
The Myth: Keeping the flowers trimmed back will increase the yield of your plants.

The Truth: So, if this were true, that means you could have a world full of virgins and we'd still have a population explosion. Man, you need every flower your plants can produce because of possible flower drop when the weather gets hot. Otherwise you'll have no chile pods, no virgins to deflower, nada.

6. Saving Seeds Saves Money!
The Myth: Save all the seeds from your garden and plant them the following year, saving money on seeds and bedding plants.

The Truth: You're gonna let your un-neutered collie and a bulldog frolic together? Check out the pups they produce—a buncha mutts! Chiles are totally like dogs (or college students on spring break…ah, good times), cross-breeding prolifically without human interference. If you want pure seed, you'll have to cage your chile plants with fabric tougher than cheesecloth to keep the bees and other insects off the flowers. Total bummer! It's all about purity, dude…that's the difference between growing chronic and schwag.

7. Jalapeños Love Bell Peppers
The Myth: Jalapeños planted next to Bells will make the Bells hot *the same year.*

The Truth: Let it never be said that I'm opposed to vegetable love, but if peppers growing next to each other can affect heat levels, then Madonna standing on stage next to Ziggy Marley makes her kids Rastas. Not likely, man.

8. Certified Seeds of Proven Varieties Will Always Produce Perfect Fruit!
The Myth: Chile breeders strive to perfection so the pods are uniform on their varieties.

The Truth: You know, my mom thought all her kids would be perfect and normal, then she had me. I mean, there's nothing about me that a good spliff won't fix, but chile genetics can also go awry. Sometimes the results will totally freak you out.

9. Hatch Chile is the Best There Is!
The Myth: Since produce vendors and fiery foods manufacturers always seem to feature Hatch chiles, it must be the best chile.

The Truth: I hate to harsh your buzz, but Hatch chile is a total myth—it simply does not exist. There is no variety called 'Hatch' and there's not enough acreage around tiny Hatch, New Mexico (population 1,647) to grow all the New Mexican chile that is supposed to be from Hatch. The number one crop grown around Hatch is alfalfa. I bet the number two crop is kush, but you didn't hear it from me.

10. New Mexico's State Vegetables Must Be, Uh, Vegetables!
The Myth: The legislators knew what they were doing when they named the chile pepper and the pinto bean as co-state vegetables.

The Truth: Dude, that was pretty stupid. "Co-State Crops" would make make more sense, because chiles are fruits and beans are legumes—neither is a vegetable like, say, arugula, or rutabaga—wait a minute, that's a root!

What is the Official State Pepper of Texas?
In 1995, the jalapeño pepper was named Texas' state vegetable, along with the pinto bean. Of course, neither are vegetables, but Dammit, Jim, they're politicians, not farmers. In the United States,

The United States of Spice

approximately 5,500 acres are under cultivation, with Texas the leading state for jalapeño production, followed by New Mexico. In 1997 the chiltepin was designated as the state's official native pepper.

Are There GMO Chile Peppers?

Not yet. But there's concern that the New Mexico chile crop is in such a downward spiral that something extreme might be needed to save it. Imports from Mexico and China, along with rising labor costs and environmental factors have put the whole industry at risk. Over the last 20 years, New Mexico has seen a 75 percent decline in the number of acres of chile grown.

Scientists at New Mexico State University's Chile Pepper Institute have been studying the genetic makeup of chile peppers for years, though no genetically modified plants have yet been created—other than those coming from natural cross-breeding. Not everyone is thrilled by the GMO idea, as it brings up the possible legal issues surrounding patented seed lines, health concerns from consumers, and headaches for traditional chile farmers who want to keep their varieties pure.

Which States Grow the Most Chiles?

Here they are, in order of production volume for 2010. Amounts are in hundredweight (CWT); 1 ton equals 1000 cwt. Also shown is the market value of that state's crop. These statistics do not include bell peppers, which are tracked in separate tables (besides, they're barely chile peppers anyway):

1. California, 2.4 million cwt, worth $135 million
2. New Mexico, 1.6 million cwt, worth $37.2 million

The entire United States produces approximately 4.5 million cwt of chile peppers annually. 2010 was the first year that California outranked New Mexico in chile production. Florida, Arizona, and Texas round out the top five chile-growing states.

What Does It Mean That A Chile Is A "Landrace?"

Landraces are adapted varieties that have been growing in the same geographic area for hundreds of years. Pod variations within a land race are common, and sometimes the pods on the same plant have different forms. Generally, landraces are genetically diverse and are well adapted to the locations where they have been cultivated. The 'Mirasol' chile landrace from Colorado is one example. Many landraces are in danger of extinction because they are not cultivated as much as commercial chile varieties.

According to the Foods and Agriculture Organization of the United Nations, in the last century, three-quarters of our foodstuffs have disappeared from farms and gardens worldwide. In North America, at least two-thirds of the crops grown on this continent in prehistoric times can no longer be found in gardens and fields anywhere in the world; either they have been replaced by modern varieties, or the fields themselves have been developed into subdivisions, schools, industrial plants, or parks.

—From *Chasing Chiles: Hot Spots Along the Pepper Trail* by Kurt Michael Friese, Kraig Kraft, and Gary Paul Nabhan

New Mexico Chile Going, Going, Gone?

It could happen. According to the NM Chile Association, the chile pepper industry is in a steep decline: 34,500 acres were harvested in 1992, but only 8,800 were harvested in 2010. Competition from other countries is on the rise: for instance, China is trying to corner the world oleoresin market, which accounts for 30% of New Mexico's chile acreage. Imports account for about 82% of chile consumed in the U.S., and unless growers find a way to reverse this trend, it doesn't look good for

Chile being roasted at the Hatch Chile Festival. If you want to be absolutely sure the chile you're eating is from Hatch, plan a trip to the festival and buy a bushel! Photo by Harald Zoschke

The United States of Spice

New Mexico chile. Sometimes chile is sold labeled as "Hatch" or "NM Grown" when it comes from outside New Mexico, or even the United States.

Chile Fraud in the Chile State?

Evildoers beware: a new 2011 law is taking aim at those who fraudulently assert that their chile is grown in New Mexico.

"What we've got is people coming in and selling chile and saying it's from New Mexico, and some of it is being shipped in from Mexico or elsewhere," said State Representative Andy Nuñez, a former chile farmer from Hatch and sponsor of the New Mexico Chile Advertising Act. "We're trying to keep the integrity of New Mexico chile, which we think is the best."

The law makes it illegal to sell or advertise any product as New Mexico chile unless its peppers are grown in the state.

Oy Vey! Chilly Chiles Developed in Israel

Did you know that peppers are Israel's leading vegetable export? That's $80 million in exports from the 2004-2005 growing season. Much of the country's pepper research and development happens at the Hebrew University of Jerusalem, where a research team has developed genetically enhanced hybrid peppers that have been raised to produce high yields when nighttime temperatures dip as low as 50 degrees Fahrenheit; previous hybrids could not survive at temperatures lower than 65 degrees Fahrenheit.

The peppers were developed as part of a large-scale experiment involving more than 25,000 plants per year, grown in southern Israel and southern Spain. The plants' increased tolerance to lower temperatures expands the geographic range in which they can be cultivated. In particular, the development opens up new areas of countries like Mexico and China to winter pepper cultivation.

What's the Earliest Known Cultivation of Chiles?

Chile peppers have long been popular in both horticultural and culinary circles – they're believed to have been cultivated in different parts of Latin America as far back as 5200 B.C.

Is There A Mild Habanero?

The Chile Breeding Project of New Mexico State University developed two non-pungent cultivars of *Capsicum chinense*, the species to which habaneros belong. Each 'NuMex Suave Orange' plant can yield up to 100 mildly pungent fruits that rate at around 835 units on the scoville scale. The word *suave* is Spanish for mellow, smooth or mild. The pods have the classic habanero flavor profile with citrusy overtones and a fruity aroma.

Formerly, plant breeders wishing to insert genes for non-pungency to modify hot chiles used them from bell peppers. But some varieties of *C. chinense* are completely non-pungent, and their genes have been used to create low-pungency fruits with the typical habanero flavor and aroma. 'NuMex Suave Red' is rated at about 500 Scoville Heat Units–about the same range as the milder New Mexican varieties.

Who is the Father of the U.S. Mexican Food Industry?

That would be Fabian Garcia, a pioneering New Mexico State University chile breeder. During more than 50 years at NMSU, Garcia carried out a series of revolutionary horticultural experiments. In 1899, he began research to develop more standardized chile varieties. Early in the 1900s, he released New Mexico 9, the first variety with a dependable pod size and heat level. The new pod variety opened commercial markets for New Mexico chile peppers and established the state's chile pepper food industry. Fifty years after his death, Garcia was inducted into the National Hall of Fame for the American Society for Horticultural Science. According to Dr. Paul Bosland of the Chile Pepper Institute, "All New Mexican-type chile peppers grown today, including the Anaheim, owe their genetic base to Fabian Garcia's New Mexico No. 9 variety."

Sombreros off to Fabian Garcia!

Of Chiles, Wheat Aphids, and Bureaucracy

It all started innocently enough. Rick Ihler of Holly Farms in Filer, Idaho casually mentioned to a Pocatello newspaper reporter that he used a combination of garlic oil and chile powder to control Russian wheat aphids on his carrot farm.

The article was published and Ilher was then called on the carpet by the Environmental Protection Agency and the Idaho Department of Agriculture. His offense? Advocating the use of a material as a pesticide that is not a registered pesticide.

Bob Spencer, chief of pesticide compliance for the Idaho Department of Agriculture said that no charges were filed against Ihler, and that the state was not considering filing any. He pointed out that even organic materials, if they are used as a pesticide, must be registered as such.

Ihler must now fill out thirteen official forms to get his mixture registered as a pesticide, despite the fact that the separate ingredients in his chile concoction have passed all the tests required by the EPA's certification program. However, even if Ihler gets it registered, he can't promote it because he's not a licensed pesticide consultant!

Ihler said he has no intention of marketing his wheat aphid treatment, and that his only interest is protecting the environment.

But wait! Fred Melton of Jacksonville, Florida, grew a jalapeño plant twelve feet, three inches tall that produced over 1700 pods. The plant was certified for the 1993 *Guinness Book of World Records* when it was a mere ten feet, six inches tall.

Under ideal conditions, a chile plant can grow to a massive size. Illustration by Kelli Bergthold

Texas or Florida: Whose Chile is Bigger?

When I was editor of *Chile Pepper* Magazine back in the day, people used to send me all sorts of crazy stuff. Sam Bravenec from Houston, Texas described a massive chile plant on his property: "I have enclosed a photograph of a pepper plant growing in my garden. This plant is now over 7 feet tall with a width of 5 feet. Every week it has at least 4 pounds of peppers waiting to be harvested. I think it originated from the original chile piquin growing in my back yard. The peppers from this plant grow to about 1 1/2 inches long and are about as hot as habanero peppers I have experienced." Surely this is the biggest chile plant ever.

Does Environment Affect Chile Heat Levels?

It has long been assumed

that about eighty percent of the heat level is fixed genetically and the remainder is determined by environmental factors. But some experts believe that the environment plays a much larger role than was originally assumed.

The questions arise because of apparently declining heat levels of domestically-grown habaneros. In recent high performance liquid chromatography tests at New Mexico State University, California orange habaneros have been measuring about 80,000 Scoville Units—far less than the 250,000 level of Habs from the Yucatán Peninsula, which were the progenitors of the domestic Habs.

Scientists have long known that stress factors—such as too little or too much water—can dramatically increase the capsaicin levels in the pods. But now they suspect that other environmental factors are operating as well, such as soil composition and pH, relative humidity, amount of ultraviolet radiation, fertilizers, and day and night temperatures. Therefore, chiles grown under near-perfect conditions would be milder than clones cultivated under stress.

How Many Species of Chiles Are There?

There are five domesticated species of peppers, dozens of pod types within those species, and hundreds of varieties within the types. An example is "NuMex Big Jim," which is a variety of the New Mexican pod type of the *Capsicum annuum* species. While the *annuum* species has many distinct types and varieties that have been named (Jalapeño, Bell, Serrano, etc.), the other species' nomenclature is less developed. The species *baccatum* is generically called "Ají," *chinense* is called "Habanero," *frutescens* is called "Tabasco," and *pubescens* is called "Rocoto."

There is great pod type diversity within these other species, but most types have not been scientifically named. Many have local names that are unfamiliar to most of us. For example, although the entire *chinense* species is generically called Habanero (the name in Mexico), different pod types of this species have local names, such as Scotch bonnet in Jamaica, 'Bhut Jolokia' in India, datil in St. Augustine, goat pepper in the Bahamas, congo pepper in Trinidad, chombo in Panama, mutton pepper in Belize, and *pimenta do cheiro* in Brazil. As with the *annuums*, the *chinense* species has many different pod shapes and varying heat levels. It is just as inaccurate to call the entire *chinense* species "habanero" as it is to call the entire *annuum* species "jalapeño." Confused yet?

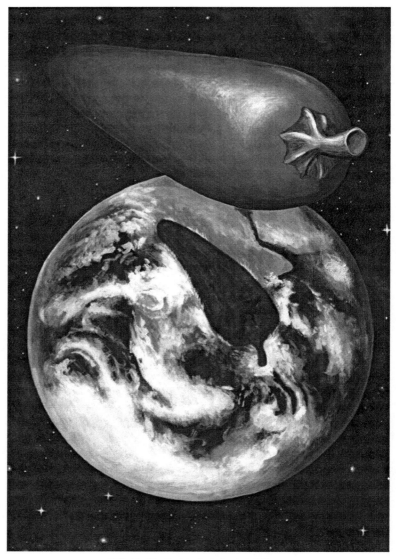

"A World of Heat" original painting by Lois Manno

Part III

A Wacky World Tour

People always want it hotter; that's the reason
habaneros caught on.

—Habanero grower Jeff Campbell

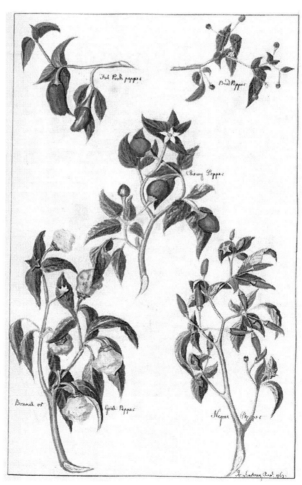

Jamaican chiles as illustrated by Rev. John Lindsay, 1767
Courtesy of the Sunbelt Archives

Dave DeWitt's Chile Trivia

Chapter 7

Caribbean History, Legend, and Lore

I love the Caribbean islands and just cannot stay away. During the past forty years, I've have explored the West Indies by jets, prop planes, seaplanes, cruise ships, yachts, buses, cars, and even on foot in some cases. Of course, I've not visited every single island and country, but my favorite hot and spicy culinary memories include:

• Finding a twelve-foot-tall kitchen pepper plant at the Good Hope Great House in Jamaica.

• Carefully trying a goat pepper-infused conch salad in a small restaurant in Nassau, Bahamas.

• Cooking with chefs in various locations in Jamaica while shooting Heat Up Your Life, my three-part video documentary on chiles.

• Catching, grilling, and devouring freshly caught yellowtail snapper with coconut and Melinda's hot sauce on the tiny island of Ambergris Caye, Belize.

• Examining Congo pepper fields in Trinidad that were adjacent to marijuana fields.

• Getting burned out on flying fish with incredibly hot piri-piri sauce aboard the *Jolly Roger* in Barbados.

• Tasting the spiced-up beach food at Magen's Bay on St. Thomas.

• Sampling jerk pork right off the grill at the Double V Jerk Center in Ocho Rios, Jamaica and learning the cook's barbecuing techniques.

One of my favorite food conversations took place at the Cheapside Market in Bridgetown, Barbados, and it taught me not to make assumptions about racial terms in the islands. At the stand of one griz-zled old man, I spotted a jar of small, thin peppers.

"Bird peppers?" I asked the vendor.

"Nigger peppers," insisted the vendor, who was a black man.

"Not a very polite term," I observed. The man just shrugged. I bought the jar.

"They're bird peppers in Trinidad but nigger peppers here," explained Anne Marie Whitaker later. "Nobody thinks anything about the word."

Indeed. Later, I asked our driver Emerson, and he just laughed. "Nigger peppers is what they are." I decided to drop the subject.

> Although jerk pork originally led the field, jerk chicken is now the most popular. In Kingston the demand for jerk chicken on the weekends is incredible. The steel drums converted to grills are ubiquitous. They line the streets and, on weekends in certain sections of Red Hills Road, so much smoke emerges from the line of drums that, except for the smell, one could be forgiven for thinking that a San Franciscan fog had come to Jamaica.
>
> —*Advice for 19th Century Tourists*
> *Who Wish to Cook Poultry*

What is Jerk Sauce?

Jamaican jerk sauces are a combination of spices and Scotch bonnet chiles used as a marinade and baste for grilled meats. The word "jerk" is thought to have originated from the word *ch?arki* (the question mark is part of the word), a Quecha word from Peru. The Spanish converted the term to *charqu*, which means jerked or dried meat. In English it became known as "jerk" and "jerky."

The technique of jerking was originated by the Maroons, Jamaican slaves who escaped from the British during the invasion of 1655 and hid in the maze of jungles and limestone sinkholes known as the Cock-pit Country. The Maroons seasoned the pork and cooked it until it was dry and would keep well in the humid tropics. During the 20th century, the technique gained enormous popularity in Jamaica and today "jerk pork shacks" are commonly found all over Jamaica. The method has evolved, however, and the pork is no longer overcooked. In addition to pork, heavily spiced chicken, fish, and beef are grilled to juicy perfection. Today there are dozens of brands of jerk sauces manufactured in Jamaica and the United States.

Is a Habanero the Same as a Scotch Bonnet Pepper?

Yes—and it's the same as a goat pepper, rocotillo, Congo pepper, etc. Here's a list of the various common names used for *Capsicum chinense* peppers in the Caribbean and the Americas.

Name	Location
7-pot	Trinidad
ají chombo	Panama
ají yaquitania	Brazil
bonda man Jacques	Martinique, Guadeloupe
booney or bonney pepper	Barbados
cachucha (or ají cachucha)	Cuba
charapilla	Peru
chile blanco	Caribbean
chinchi-uchu	Peru
Congo pepper	Trinidad
le derriere de Madame Jacques	Guadeloupe
Dominica pepper	U.S. Virgin Islands
fatalii	Caribbean, Africa
goat pepper, billy goat pepper	Bahamas, Africa

Tending pork at the Jerk Centre, Jamaica. Photo 1994 by Dave DeWitt

A Wacky World Tour

Guinea pepper	Caribbean
habanero	Mexico, Belize
moruga	Trinidad
murici	Brazil
panameño	Costa Rica
panco	Peru
piment bouc	Haiti
pimenta-de-bode	Brazil
pimenta do cheiro	Brazil
rocotillo	Peru, Caribbean
scorpion	Trinidad
Scotch bonnet	Jamaica and Caribbean
tiger tooth	Guyana

The Naughty Derriere of Peppers

A Caribbean natural pepper remedy supposedly will spice up your love life! In Guadeloupe, where the *chinense* species is called *le derriere de Madame Jacques*, that pepper is combined with crushed peanuts, cinnamon sticks, nutmeg, vanilla beans packed in brandy, and an island liqueur called Creme de Banana—considered to be an aphrodisiac. We assume it's taken internally.

Real Men Eat Cock Soup

"It appears that there must be a presiding officer at a curry goat feed. He sat at the head of the table and directed the fun. There was a story-telling contest, bits of song, reminiscences that were humorous pokes and gibes at each other. All of this came with the cock soup. This feast is so masculine that chicken soup would not be allowed. It must be soup from roosters. After the cock soup comes ram goat and rice. No nanny goat in this meal either. It is ram goat or nothing." –American folklorist and anthropologist Zora Neale Hurston, 1939

Jamaica's Colorful Food Names

"Yet so many sojourners in the Jamaican island paradise are deprived. Many who have come not only once, but several times, never have an opportunity to know about ackees. Nobody bothers to introduce them to Solomon Gundy or to Stamp and Go (better known among the islanders as Stamps), or to Stand and Rock or Dip-And-Fall-Back. Year after year, some people return yet nobody tells them how a green banana should be dipped into a Mackerel Run-Down. Perhaps they never even hear about a Run-Down. Or Firestick Coffee. Or the big, gingery cookies called Bullas (an African word). How sad!" –South African author Poppy Cannon

Pukka Chileheads

"Busha" Howe Peter Browne served as governor of Jamaica, and his descendents are still producing sauces and condiments based on authentic recipes from the 1800s. This passage is from Busha Browne's Diary, 1837:

"Thomas, my bookkeeper, accosted me after breakfast and insisted I accompany him to his place. When we arrived it was to find his usual gaggle of some of the prettier estate girls (one of these days that lad will get himself into deep trouble) engaged in some sort of food preparation. There were mortars and pestles all around and the air was sharp with a pungent yet delightful smell. It seems that he had been doing a little experimentation of his own and had produced a Hades hot pepper sauce. He gave me a little. T'was as fiery as all Hell and would have done for the Devil himself. It was made by pulverising good quality Scotch bonnets with a little vinegar. Since it was indeed the real thing, we decided there and then to call it Pukka Sauce. A fitting name we also thought for those pukka people who like their food and other things hot and spicy."

A Scotch Bonnet Fable

A West Indian folk tale tells of a Creole woman who loved the fragrant island pods so much that she decided to make a soup out of them. She

Bake and Shark Stand, Trinidad. Notice the interesting food names on the sign.
1992 photo by Mary Jane Wilan

reasoned that since the Scotch bonnets were so good in other foods, a soup made just of them would be heavenly. But after her children tasted the broth, it was so blisteringly hot that they ran to the river to cool their mouths. Unfortunately, they drank so much water that they drowned! The moral of the story is to be careful with Scotch bonnets and their relatives, which is why many sauce companies combine them with vegetables or fruits to dilute the heat. And water, of course, is hardly the best cool-down; dairy products are.

Caribbean Peppers Get Sauced

One of the most common uses for hot peppers in the Caribbean is in hot sauces. The Carib and Arawak Indians used pepper juice for seasoning.

After the "discovery" of chile peppers by Europeans, slave-ship captains combined pepper juice with palm oil, flour, and water to make a "slabber sauce" that was served over ground beans to the slaves aboard the ship. The most basic hot sauces on the islands were made by soaking chopped Scotch bonnets in vinegar (making pepper pickles) and then sprinkling the fiery vinegar on foods. Over the centuries, each island developed its own style of hot sauce by combining the crushed chiles with other ingredients such as mustard, fruits, or tomatoes.

The Caribbean Haggis

Jug Jug is one of those great Caribbean dishes that claims a long history. It is a Barbadian dish usually made at Christmas time; some call it "transported haggis" in memory of the Scots who, after being exiled to Barbados after the Monmouth Rebellion of 1685, created a Caribbean version of their beloved haggis. The Caribbean recipe differs in several respects from the original haggis: Instead of stuffing the filling inside a sheep's stomach lining along with a minced mixture of the animal's organs, Barbadians use minced meat and mold the mixture in a bowl. Another difference: Islanders use either Guinea corn flour, cornmeal, or millet instead of the traditional Scots cereal oats. And what would a island dish be without the addition of hot peppers?

Chapter 7 Chile Quiz : Caribbean Chile Dishes

Match Column 1 with Column 2.

1. **Souse** **A.** East Indian hot and spicy sweet pickle that is popular in the Caribbean.

2. **Buss-up-shut** **B.** A Jamaican soup with goat meat, Scotch bonnets, and white rum.

3. **Chutney**   **C.** A hot and spicy East Indian mango relish.

4. **Kucheela**   **D.** In the eastern Caribbean, a dish made with salted fish and seasoned with lime, chiles, tomatoes, and onions.

5. **Buljol**   **E.** A popular Sunday breakfast dish in Trinidad and Barbados that is made from spicy pickled pork parts.

6. **Mannish water F.** A flaky bread served with curries.

Michael Coelho and Dave DeWitt in the herb fields of Paramin, Trinidad. The slopes are so steep, some chile fields are nearly vertical. 1992 photo by Mary Jane Wilan

A Wacky World Tour

82

The chile is the same as the needle: equal sharpness.

Don't be afraid of the chile, even though it is so red.

We eat this food because our ancestors came from Hell.

—Mexican Chile Proverbs

Detail of a Mural at the Palacio Nacional in Mexico City: *Vendors in the Tlatelolco Market* by Diego Rivera, c. 1930.

Chapter 8

Ancestors from Hell: Mexico and Latin America

It has often been written that the only national cuisine of Mexico is the cuisine of chile, and the fact that I've been to Mexico ten times more than to any other country is testament to that. I've spent considerable time in Mexico, from watching the Sonoran chiltepín harvest in La Aurora, to collecting chilhuacle chiles at the stand of Eliseo Ramirez in the mercado in Oaxaca, to cooking with a chef on the beach at the Ritz-Carlton Hotel in Cancún. For my 3-part video documentary, *Heat Up your Life*, we shot in five locations in Mexico, and I remember the peacocks walking in front of the camera in Cuernavaca. In Costa Rica, we visited the 'Rica Red' habanero fields in the aptly named town of Los Chiles.

One of my favorite culinary experiences in Mexico was when Chef Dany of the Hotel California in Todos Santos, Baja California Sur, took me on a non-touristy fishing trip with local commercial fishermen aboard an old ponga boat. We had great luck, and after we coasted back up on the beach, Dany instructed the captain about the fish, and soon 33-pounds of clean fillets were delivered to Dany's new restaurant, Santo Vino. In a matter of minutes, Dany had invited 18 lucky people to a private fish feast that evening and served fish that were only five or six hours out of the ocean. The first course was Mexican Sashimi (my name for it), spiced up with serrano chiles, and I've never seen so much raw fish devoured so quickly. That course was soon followed by grilled grouper topped with a savory sauce. The wine flowed, the conversations were animated, and it was the perfect end to a truly wonderful day of fishing.

> This plant (the Chiltepin), used ceremonially and privately, is thought to drive away approaching sickness. The man who does not eat chile is immediately suspected of being a sorcerer.
> —a Tarahumara Indian quoted by Wendell Bennett
> in his book, *The Tarahumara:*
> *An Indian Tribe of Northern Mexico.*

> Chiles were as significant when they were absent as when they were present. The concepts, familiar to Europeans, of fasting and penance were widespread in Mesoamerica, and without exception the basic penance was to deny oneself salt and chile.
> —Author Sophie Coe

Chiles for the Spirit World

Among the descendants of the Maya, chile is regarded as a powerful agent to ward off spells. For the Tzotzil Indians of the Chiapas highlands, chile assists in both life and death. The hot pods are rubbed on the lips of newborn infants and are burned during the funeral ceremonies of *viejos* ("old ones") to defeat evil spirits that might be around. The Huastec tribe of San Carlos Potosi and Vera Cruz treat victims of the "evil eye" with chile peppers. An egg is dipped in ground chile and then rubbed on the victim's body to return the pain to the malefactor.

Chiles of the Gods

One reason for the popularity of pods was that the Incas worshipped the chile pepper as one of the four brothers of their creation myth. "Agar-Uchu," or "Brother Chile Pepper," was believed to be the brother of the first Incan king. Garcilaso de la Vega observed that the chile pods were perceived to symbolize the teachings of the early Incan brothers. Chile peppers were thus regarded as holy plants, and the Incas' most rigorous fasts were those prohibiting all chiles. The Aymaras, an Andean tribe conquered by the Incas in the fifteenth century, had a saying that went: "Am I your salt or chile that you always have me in your mouth and speak ill of me?"

While not overt, the influence of the chiltepin can be seen throughout the Sonoran Desert region. Tables are set with small bowls of dried chiltepin to crumble on top of the plate of the day. The baseball team of Baviacora, in the Rio Sonora Valley, is called the Chiltepineros. During years of plenty, impromptu stands and speed-bump merchants hawk their wares. Chiltepines can be found on amulets to ward away spirits and in herbal cures. Much like trying to find the chiltepin plants in the desert, it takes and adjustment of vision to see the chiltepin in Sonoran daily life. But once you get that chile vision homed in, you'll see it everywhere you go.

—Kraig Craft, co-author of
Chasing Chiles: Hot Spots Along the Pepper Trail

Chiltepins, the wild pods sacred to the Tarahumara and other Latin American cultures.
Photo by Jeffrey Gerlach

A Wacky World Tour

The Mayans Loved Their Chiles

By the time the Mayas reached the peak of their civilization in southern Mexico and the Yucatán Peninsula, around A.D. 500, they had a highly developed system of agriculture. Maize was their most important crop, followed closely by beans, squash, chiles, and cacao. Perhaps as many as thirty different varieties of chiles were cultivated, and they were sometimes planted in plots by themselves but more often in fields already containing tomatoes and sweet potatoes. There were three species of chiles grown by the Maya and their descendants in Central America: *annuum*, *chinense*, and *frutescens*—and they were all imports from other regions. The *annuums* probably originated in Mexico, while the *frutescens* came from Panama, and the *chinense* from the Amazon Basin via the Caribbean.

The Aztecs Skipped Sex and Chiles for the Gods

In 1529, Bernardino de Sahagún, a Spanish Franciscan friar living in Nueva España (Mexico) noted that the Aztecs ate hot red or yellow chile peppers in their hot chocolate and in nearly every dish they prepared! Father Sahagún, one of the first behavioral scientists, also noted that chiles were revered as much as sex by the ancient Aztecs. While fasting to appease their rather bloodthirsty gods, the priests required two abstentions by the faithful: sexual relations and chile peppers. Read more about the aphrodisiacal properties of chiles in chapter 13, The Passionate Pepper.

The Aztecs Had Their Own Heat Scale

According to Joseph Sheppard, Ph.D., a specialist in Mesoamerican cooking, the Aztecs had a whole slew of words to describe various levels of spice in their food. Here's the Nahuatl scale for the "burning within" sensation (iticococ):

cococ: hot
cocopatic: very hot
cocoquauitl: extremely hot
cocopetztic: glistening hot
cocopetzpatic: very glistening hot
cocopetzquauitl: extremely glistening hot

A Spanish Lust for Chiles

Chile peppers were such a novelty to the Spanish explorers in Mexico that rumors were rampant about their medical properties. The Jesuit priest, poet, and historian, José de Acosta, wrote in 1590, "Taken moderately, chile helps and comforts the stomach for digestion." The priest

undoubtedly had heard rumors about the reputed aphrodisiac quali-
ties of chiles because he continued his description of chile with the
following warning: "But if they take too much, it has bad effects, for
of itself it is very hot, fuming, and pierces greatly, so the use thereof is
prejudicial to the health of young folks, chiefly to the soul, for it pro-
vokes to lust." Despite the good father's suspicions, the only thing lust-
ful about chiles was the desire everyone had to devour them, including
the Spanish.

What is in *Mole* Sauce?

Mole sauces originated in the state of Oaxaca, Mexico and can have
dozens of ingredients. The list varies, depending on whether you're
creating a green, red, or black *mole* sauce. Known as The Julia Child of
Mexican Cooking, Diana Kennedy's recipe for *Mole Negro Oaxaqueno*
(Black Oaxacan *Mole*), which appears in her landmark 440-page tome
Oaxaca al Gusto, includes the following ingredients:

Chilhuacles negros	Garlic
Mulato chiles	Cinnamon
Pasilla chiles	Peppercorns
Chipotle mora chiles	Cloves
Pork lard	Cumin seeds
Oaxacan drinking chocolate	Mexican oregano
Sesame seeds	Thyme
Peanuts	Marjoram
Almonds	Bay leaves
Walnuts	Sugar
Pecans	Salt
Raisins	
Plantain	
Semisweet rolls	
Onion	

Are Chiles Muy Caliente?

No. In Spanish, *Caliente* means
something is hot from physical fire, so irons and motors
become *caliente*, not chiles.
Picante implies something hot
from spice and is the word of
choice. However, *picante* is
not commonly used by *rurales*

(country folk.) *Picoso* is more often used to imply hot from spice. This comes from *picar*, meaning to prick or to sting. *Pico de gallo* is a famous salsa using the word *picar*, and the polite translation implies the sting from the peck of a rooster. Most *rurales*, however, use still another word for hot and spicy food. Most often they say *enchiloso*. This is from *enchilarse*, meaning to "enchile" something. If food is *enchiloso*, they often times exclaim *"Me enchil,"* or "I enchiladed myself." Confused yet?

Tabasco® Grows Its Peppers in Mexico

Central America is becoming quite a chile pepper growing mecca. The McIlhenny Company of Avery Island, Louisiana, grows the majority of Tabasco® peppers for its famous sauce in Mexico, Honduras, and Colombia. Costa Rica is the source of habaneros and other chiles for hot sauces, and there are substantial growing operations in Panama and Guatemala.

Secrets of Mole

"A *mole* recipe is not something dashed off on a file card and handed to an appreciative dinner guest. It is a family treasure, and in some cases a family secret. A visitor certainly can ask for the recipe and the flattered cook may begin ticking off the ingredients off the fingers of both hands, sometimes two or three times over. But ask the cook to specify proportions of ingredients and the steps to create the *mole*, and the conversation suddenly can become vague."
—Journalist William Stockton

How Many Oaxacan Moles Are There?

For the record, the seven *moles* are: *mole negro, mole coloradito, mole verde, mole amarillo, mole rojo, manchas manteles* ("tablecloth stainer"), and *mole chichilo*. They are all descendants of *clemole*, believed to be the original *mole* of Oaxaca. It was quite simple, being composed of ancho and pasilla chiles, garlic, cloves, cinnamon, and coriander.

"There may be seven *moles*," say the locals, "but thousands and thousands of cooks each has their own private version of all of the moles, so how many does that make?" One magazine writer suggested: "Oaxaca should be the land of 200 *moles*!"

A Holy *Mole* Miracle

Mole poblano, originally called *mole de olores* ("fragrant mole"), is the sauce traditionally served on special occasions such as Christmas that combines chiles and chocolate, a popular and revered food of the Aztecs. Moctezuma's court consumed fifty jugs of chile-laced hot chocolate a day, and warriors drank it to soothe their nerves before going into battle. However, the story of how chocolate was combined with chile sauces does not involve warriors, but rather nuns.

Legend holds that *mole* poblano was invented in the sixteenth century by the nuns of the convent of Santa Rosa in the city of Puebla. It seems that the archbishop was coming to visit, and the nuns were worried because they had no food elegant enough to serve someone of his eminence. So, they prayed for guidance and one of the nuns had a vision. She directed that everyone in the convent should begin chopping and grinding everything edible they could find in the kitchen. Into a pot went chiles, tomatoes, nuts, sugar, tortillas, bananas, raisins, garlic, avocados, and dozens of herbs and spices. The final ingredient was the magic one: chocolate. The chocolate, they reasoned, would smooth the flavor of the sauce by slighly cutting its heat. Then the nuns slaughtered their only turkey and served it with the *mole* sauce to the archbishop, who declared it the finest dish he had ever tasted.

What's A Chipotle?
The word "chipotle" comes from the Nahuatl word *chilpoktli,* meaning "smoked chile pepper."

While pretty much any chile can be smoke-dried, all chipotle peppers start out as jalapeños. Most jalapeño chiles are harvested in their green, immature, phase. Others are harvested later when they turn bright red, but others are left on the plant. When the last jalapeños are deep red and have lost much of their moisture, they are made into chipotles.

After harvest, the pods are smoked for several days until completely dry. Traditionally this was done over a wood fire, but modern methods include industrial gas-powered dryers.

Chinese Imports Threaten Mexican Chile Industry
Chinese de Arbol chiles? Chinese anchos? Yes, imported Chinese chiles that mimic the same popular Mexican varieties are hurting Mexican chile farmers because they are cheaper. One Mexican chile vendor in the main

A chipotle is a smoke-dried jalapeño.
Photo by Harald Zoschke

market in Mexico City, sells twice the number of imported bags of chiles as he does the domestic ones. Arturo Lomeli, author of *El Chile y Otros Picantes*, wrote: "Chile, they say is the soul of the Mexicans—a nutrient, a medicine, a drug, a comfort. For many Mexicans, if it were not for the existence of chile, their national identity would begin to disappear." Chinese chiles now account for one-third of all dried peppers consumed in Mexico.

"The Chinese are winning at everything. Now they're beating us at chile peppers, too," said Miguel Angel Romo, a seller of dried peppers at Mexico City's Central de Abastos market.

The Ají Monolith

About A.D. 900, a sculptor of the Chavin culture in Peru carved elaborate designs into a sharp-pointed granite shaft measuring eight feet long and a foot wide, which has become known as the Tello Obelisk. The principal figure on this obelisk is a mythical creature, the black caiman. The sharp point of the stone corresponds to a real caiman's narrow snout, and the end of the stone is carved with the feet and claws of the reptile, which appear to be holding the leaves and pods of a chile plant. As yet, no scholar has deciphered the meaning of a magical caiman grasping chile peppers in its claws, but the image is suggestive of the magical powers that the people of the Andes believed were inherent in the powerful pods.

The Chiles of Chile

Although the habanero relatives of the *chinense* species of the *Capsicum* genus do occasionally appear in the Andes, the two major chiles of choice in the region are ajís

This drawing of the Tello Obelisk shows what appears to be a head sprouting chile pods (lower right hand corner).
The drawing is a reconstruction by Dr. Peter G. Rowe, Professor of Anthropology at the University of Delaware.

and rocotos. The *baccatum* species, familiarly termed "ají" throughout South America, originated either in Bolivia or in Peru and, according to archaeological evidence, was probably domesticated in Peru about 2,500 B.C.

Salsa Has Ancient Roots

The remains of seven different varieties of chiles found in a cave in the state of Oaxaca, Mexico led researcher Linda Perry to theorize that early farmers were eating the early forms of salsa. Perry is a scientist with the Smithsonian Institution who developed the technique of determining the type of plants in ancient bowls by analyzing starch grains found in their residue. Three decades ago, archaeological materials and artifacts were found in Guila Naquitz cave near Mitla by University of Michigan archaeologist Kent Flannery. They were never analyzed until Perry perfected her technique. Then Flannery sent the artifacts to Perry. She theorized that the chiles were being ground up with other ingredients such as tropical fruits to make a "proto-salsa." She noted: "Archaeologists have always felt that chile peppers were very important and became important early."

Perry believed that the farmers along a nearby river were using the caves for shelter and eating. "What was interesting to me was that we were able to determine that they were using the peppers both dried and fresh," Perry said. (Chiles broken while fresh have a recognizable breakage pattern.) "It shows us that ancient Mexican food was very much like today. They would have used fresh peppers in salsas or in immediate preparation, and they would have used the dried peppers to toss into stews or to grind up into sauces like moles."

Stalking the Flaming Canary

Food writer and adventurer Robb Walsh reported on his encounter with canary chiles: The, which is found in limited quantities in the Oaxaca and Michoacán areas of Mexico, is the only member of the species *Capsicum pubescens* found in North America. At first glance, the pods look much like habanero chiles. They are found green, but more often they are bright yellow or orange, hence the name: canary peppers. However, there is no mistaking the canario for the habanero once you've cut one open—the seeds of the canario, like all members of the *pubescens* species, are always black. The plant itself is also impossible to mistake: *Capsicum pubescens* features purple flowers and dark purplish stalks that are covered with hairy fuzz.

The chile canario is usually roasted, cut into strips and combined with lengthwise slices of raw onion and moistened with lime juice.

A Wacky World Tour

This salsa is traditionally served with *totopos*, the Oaxaqueño version of tortilla chips. The chile canario is very thick-walled and has a rich, fruity flavor when roasted. Whether eaten raw or roasted, canarios are hot, but nowhere near as hot as habaneros. The mystery of the canario pepper is how this lone member of the South American rocoto family came to grow in North America. Does it represent the beginning of a northward spread of the species *Capsicum pubescens*? If so, why are the recipes for its use so well known among the Zapotec Indians of Oaxaca? Could the chile canario be the last vestige of an "endangered species," an old strain of *Capsicum* that is dying out in North America?

Workers harvest habaneros near Merida, Yucatan, Mexico. Photo courtesy of Sunbelt Archives

There are only three restrictions on hot pepper use in Peru. They are not eaten by small children, nursing mothers, or the sick. It is common to hear doctors putting patients *en dieta*, which is nothing more than a temporary ban on ají and rocoto consumption. As a punitive measure, thumbsucking toddlers may have the offending finger dipped in ají juice, but more than one Peruvian, laughing, will theorize that this only serves to start the ají addiction.

—Journalist Mary Dempsey

Chiles as Change

Food was not the only use for the beloved chiles of the Incas. According to historian L.E. Valcercel, chile peppers were so highly valued in Inca society that they were probably used as currency. Since there were no coins or bills in those days, certain preferred products like chiles became part of a rudimentary monetary system. He noted that until the mid-twentieth century, shoppers in the plaza of Cuzco could buy goods with *rantii*, a handful of chiles.

Chile Quiz for Chapter 8: Mexican Chile Varieties Beginning with "C"
Match Column 1 with Column 2

1. Capone	**A.** A yellow variety of the rocoto, or chile manzano.
2. Corazón.	**B.** A variety of chiltepín in Veracruz.
3. Canario	**C.** In Jalisco, Nayarit, and Aguascalientes, a variety of de árbol.
4. Cola de Rata	**D.** A cultivated variety of cascabel grown in Nayarit.
5. Chilpaya	**E.** A spicy, heart-shaped poblano grown in Durango.
6. Cuauhchilli	**F.** An emasculated chile; one with the seeds removed.
7. Cora	**G.** A term for a long, thin variety of chile de árbol in Nayarit.

Chile peppers are obviously extremely important in Ethiopian curries, and they have even inspired a derogatory expression, *ye wend alich a*, meaning a man who has no pepper in him.

—20th century Afrikaner author
Laurens van der Post

Peri peri chile from Africa. Photo courtesy of Sunbelt Archives

Dave DeWitt's Chile Trivia

Chapter 9

Adventures In Hottest Africa

As editor of two magazines and the SuperSite,

I learned a lot about African food and cooking from the articles I edited, and during the research I did for my book, *Flavors of Africa*. But I had never been to the continent. In 2006 I got the chance when I consulted with an attorney on a chile plant patent case and hooked up with the management of Nando's spicy chicken restaurants. Nando's now has approximately 560 restaurants in 32 countries, and they expanded to Washington, D. C. in 2007.

The flight from Amsterdam to Johannesburg covers the nearly the entire length of Africa and it was incredible to see the terrain slowly change from the dunes of the Sahara to the rain forests of central Africa. We toured from Kruger National Park in the north (and had breakfast in the bush!) to Cape Town in the south, which could be the most beautiful city in the world. We stayed at the Lanzerac Manor and Winery in Stellenbosch, the wine capital of South Africa and the wine and food there was superb.

Back in Johannesburg, our guide Chris took us to a Nando's location in Parktown North, and I ordered the 1/4 chicken meal, with spicy rice. When asked if I wanted it mild, medium, or hot, of course I said "hot." After biting into a chicken thigh, I thought, "Oh crap, these peri-peri peppers are superhot and I've got to eat it all or look like a wimp to the South Africans." I managed to finish it without hiccuping and noted that the chicken itself was extremely tasty, much more so than

U.S. poultry. The chicken is marinated in hot sauce, then basted with more hot sauce as it is grilled over open flames.

My favorite culinary moment was at the lodge of Robbie Brozin, owner of Nando's. The lodge is on the Crocodile River, and I could see the hippos cavorting in it from the verandah. Beyond them was the Kruger wilderness. An excellent Nando's-infused lunch from chef Rochelle Schaetzl was served in the living room while we watched the Pretoria Blue Bulls rugby team go into action on the huge television. That was an unforgettable afternoon!

> The person who has once acquired a taste in the tropics for...African chiles becomes an addict.
> —20th century Afrikaner author Laurens van der Post

Anyone for Some Tasty, Chile-Stuffed Warthog?

Readers fascinated with Africa should be aware that there's another side to the spicy dishes of Africa. Tourists in Zimbabwe like their meals to be as exotic as their vacations, so chefs are busy serving them such delicacies as as fried flying ants, field mice casserole, sun-dried caterpillars, boiled elephant trunk, and fried crocodile tail.

"Tourists like to return home and boast they ate a crocodile," says Jan de Haast, a director of Zimbabwe's Sun Hotel Chain. "It's better than the other way around."

So far, the most popular exotic dishes have been roasts and steaks from antelope such as eland and kudu. Little of the exotic food is actually killed in the wild; most of it is bred on farms. Mark Cosyns, the head chef at Harare's Sheraton Hotel, has had great success with roast warthog. "The legs, roasted with mint or apple sauce, are particularly good," he says.

One of the least popular dishes has been the elephant trunk, which is tough, takes six hours to boil, and isn't all that tasty, according to Cosyns. "Few diners want to confront a pair of nostrils on their plate," he laments.

A Fiery Remedy

Author Harva Hatchen observed many uses for chiles in Africa: "West Africans are extremely fond of highly seasoned food. Most often the heat is generated by red peppers, used in quantities hard to believe. A home economics teacher in Lagos gave me her recipe for Pepper

Chicken, which calls for four large red peppers one tablespoon of cayenne. Red peppers have medicinal uses in West Africa, too. They are widely regarded as a cold remedy, eaten whole and uncooked, like an apple. This undoubtedly flushes out all eight sinus cavities as well as the tear ducts."

When Did Chile Peppers Come to Africa?

Chiles were unknown before 1500 but conquered a continent in less than half a century. The Africans embraced the imported Capsicums with only matched, perhaps, by the people of India and Mexico.

Since the Arabic countries north of the Sahara are linked culturally, economically, and gastronomically more closely with the Mediterranean region than with the rest of Africa, there is little doubt that chiles first appeared in North Africa. They did not spread into the rest of Africa from that region, but rather were brought by Portuguese explorers and traders. Even before Columbus, Portuguese exploration of Africa had proceeded down the west coast of the continent between 1460 and 1488. When Vasco de Gama rounded the Cape of Good Hope, crossed the Indian Ocean, and landed in India in 1498, he established the trade route for spices and other goods that the Portuguese controlled for over a century.

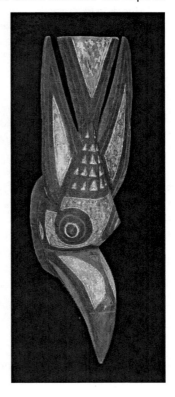

Feathered Chileheads Spread the Fire

The Portuguese may have been responsible for the introduction of chiles into Africa, but spreading them was for the birds. History—and evolution—repeated themselves. Precisely in the same manner that prehistoric chiles spread north from South to Central America, chiles conquered Africa.

African birds fell in love with chile peppers. Attracted to the brightly-colored pods, many species of African birds raided the small garden plots and then flew further inland, spreading the seeds and returning the chiles

African birds like the one portrayed in this mask were responsible for spreading chiles all over Africa.
Photo by Roman Bonnefoy

to the wild. Chiles thus became what botanists call a subspontaneous crop—newly established outside of their usual habitat, and only involuntarily spread by man.

From West Africa, birds moved the peppers steadily east, and at some time chiles either reached the coast of East Africa or met the advance of bird-spread chiles from Mozambique and Mombasa. They also spread chiles south to the Cape of Good Hope. Remember that these chiles were being spread by birds centuries before the interior of Africa was explored by Europeans. So when the early explorers encountered chiles, it was only natural for them to consider the pods to be native to Africa.

What are Chiles Called in Africa?

There are dozens, if not hundreds of names for the pungent pods of Africa. The Portuguese there call the *chile pimento*, the English refer to it as chilli, the Muslim words for it are *shatta* and *felfel*, and the French word for chile is *piment*. The Swahili words for chile are *pili-pili, piri-piri*, and *peri-peri*, which are regional variations referring to both chiles and dishes made with particularly pungent pods. Tribal names vary greatly: chile is *mano* in Liberia, *barkono* in northern Nigeria, *ata* in southern Nigeria, *sakaipilo* in Madagascar, *pujei* in Sierra Leone, *foronto* in Senegal, and the ominous *fatalii* in Central African Republic.

> Marco Polo did not visit our country. And Ethiopia was never conquered. It came under brief Italian rule during Mussolini's time, but for the most part, we did not have direct and intimate dealings with foreign powers. And Ethiopian cuisine remained a secret.
>
> —Daniel Jote Mesfin, author of
> *Exotic Ethiopian Cooking*

Bacteria Beware

"When I first arrived to work in Malindi, I was told by my sister's African Muslim driver (he's part African, part Arab/Swahili), that folk wisdom states that if I eat a chile pepper with each meal, I will never get food poisoning. As a former bus driver, he's eaten in lots of unhygenic places, and swears by this method. At first, I supposed that was because if your stomach can handle chiles, it can also handle a few bacteria. Later, I learned about the antibiotic effects of chile on bacteria, so African folk wisdom is proved by science." —Author Michelle Cox

Madagascar Heat

According to travel journalist Judith Ritter, Chef Jean-Louis Themis of L'Exotic Restaurant in Montreal, Canada was born and raised on the African island of Madagascar. He is exuberant when he talks about the role of chiles in his country's cuisine. "It's medicinal. It's an aphrodisiac. It's delicious. The pepper is king!" Madagascar grows many varieties of peppers, but the most famous is the little "bird pepper." In Malagasy (the country's language), the pepper's name is tsy lany dimy laihy. That means "even five men can't finish it."

Chile Peppers for Lion Control

With the population of Africa continuing to grow, conflict between lions and humans is a constant issue. Scientists are experimenting with ways to keep people and lions safe. They recommended that farmers in Tanzania hang chile peppers in their fields, which repel the bush pigs that lions love to eat.

Where are African Chiles Grown?

Morocco and Tunisia are the largest producers of chiles in North Africa, followed by Sudan, which sells its chiles to Egypt. Today, Nigeria and Sierra Leone are major producers of many varieties, including the moderately pungent funtua chile. In Nigeria, approximately 150,000 acres are under cultivation with chiles of all varieties, making it the largest producer of chiles in Africa, accounting for about fifty percent of all production. Most of the chile is consumed domestically, although some is exported to the United Kingdom.

What's Harissa?

Harissa is a complex and powerful paste featuring red chiles for heat and color, mixed with curry spices such as cinnamon, coriander, caraway, and cumin for flavor. Of Tunisian origin, it is used all over North Africa in the kitchen and at the table to fire up soups, stews, and less spicy curries. It is extremely hot and is used as a condiment, a marinade, a basting sauce, and as a salad dressing. Harissa is often served on the side as a dipping sauce for grilled meats such as kebabs and is also served with couscous.

Commercial Tunisian harissa sauce produced in the Cap Bon region. Photo by Rainer Zenz

West Africa: Magic and Medicine

The German explorer G. Schweinfurth reported that the natives of West Africa concocted a magic potion from wild chiles, which ensured eternal youth! Other explorers observed that chiles were used to spice up dried locusts, which were considered a tasty snack in some parts of Africa. In 1871, when the American Henry Stanley finally found the "lost" David Livingstone, he discovered that the Scottish explorer had lived on meat and gravy seasoned with wild chiles.

> I took many meals in Mombasa at the excellent—
> though cramped and crowded—Big Bite
> restaurant on Maungano Road in New Town.
> Here I found cooks using spices like painters use
> colors. They spoke little English but they were
> able to impart several recipes to me. My favorite
> was a hot sauce based on a spice blend and the
> juice of the Ukwaju, a native East African lemon.
> It's everywhere in Mombasa. The Portuguese
> are remembered for two things here: Fort Jesus
> and the *pili-pili* pepper. And when Fort Jesus is
> reduced by time and raindrops to a pile of dust,
> people will still be enjoying the *pili-pili*.
> —World traveler and author Richard Sterling

The Hottest Brides Have The Hottest Berbere

A large East African producer of chiles is Ethiopia, and most of the chiles are used domestically in their highly-spiced cuisine. The most important spice mixture is a condiment called berbere, which is made with the hottest chiles available, plus other spices, and is served as a side dish with meat, used as a coating for drying meats, or is a major ingredient of curried meats. Tribal custom dictated that berbere be served with kifto, a raw meat dish that is served warm. According to legend, the more delicious a woman's berbere was, the better chance she had to win a husband. Recipes for berbere were closely guarded, since they were a woman's secret weapon!

The Slave Curries of South Africa

The Dutch colonized South Africa because of its ideal position halfway between the Netherlands and the Spice Islands. Late in the seventeenth century, commerce between the Dutch East India Company and the new Dutch colony of South Africa picked up considerably because of an important commodity: Malay slaves, referred to in South African literature as "the king of slaves." The men were utilized as farmers, carpenters, musicians, tailors, and fishermen, while the women were expert cooks who not only introduced exotic Spice Islands dishes, but also imported the spices necessary to prepare them.

Among the Malaysian spices transferred by the slaves to South Africa were anise seed, fennel, turmeric, ginger, cardamom, cumin, coriander, mustard seed, tamarind, and garlic. Chiles, of course, were introduced by the Portuguese traders and eventually were disseminated across Africa by birds. Curiously, coconuts—so important in the Spice Islands—do not play a role in South African curries.

What are the Hottest Chiles in Africa?

Reputedly, the hottest African chiles are those called Mombassa and Uganda, which are *Capsicum chinense*, probably introduced by the Portuguese from Brazil. In some parts of Africa, these habanero-type chiles are called "crazy-mad" peppers, and, reputedly, they were re-introduced into the Caribbean islands during the slave trade.

How Curries Could Have Killed Apartheid

"The reappearance of curry in the fundamental and most conservative departments of the kitchen of the interior shows to what a depth the Indian influence spread. The best place for curries was and remains Natal. Curry in all the forms in which it is done in India is served in hotels and homes and eaten with relish, however strong the colour prejudice of the household in which they are served. If only the heart in South Africa would be governed for a year or two by the national palate, there would be no apartheid or racial prejudice left in the land, because our cooking is the best advertisement the world could possibly have for a multi-racial society, free of religious, racial, and other forms of discrimination, if not even for immediate and unbridled miscegenation." —South African author Laurens van der Post, 1977

Chapter 9 Chile Quiz: African Terms for Chile

Match Column 1 with Column 2.

1. Pujei.
2. Sakaipilo.
3. Mano.
4. Felfel al har.
5. Ata.
6. Pili-Pili.

A. Term for chile in Liberia.
B. The generic term for chiles among the Yoruba of Nigeria.
C. Arabic term for North African chiles.
D. Term for chiles in Sierra Leone.
E. Swahili term for chiles.
F. Term for hot chile pepper in Madagascar.

A Wacky World Tour

This is the famous Java curry; and if you
have taken plenty of the pepper and chutney,
and other hot things, your mouth will burn
for half an hour as though you had drunk
from a kettle of boiling water. And when you
have eaten freely of curry, you don't want
any other breakfast. Everybody eats curry
here daily, because it is said to be good for the
health by keeping the liver active, and
preventing fevers.

—Thomas Knox, *The Boy Travelers
in the Far East*, 1884

A painting of Java, circa 1872 by Abraham Salm.
Courtesy Tropenmuseum of the Royal Tropical Institute (KIT)

Chapter 10

Asia's Spiciest Islands and More

The smiling vendor in the Bangkok produce market had a black-and-white kitten sitting on a pile of green and red *prik khee nu* chiles and was surprised to see a farangi in front of her. Tourists were supposed to shop in the retail markets, not in the sprawling, riverside wholesale market, but we were on a search for chiles. And we found tons of them! Dried chiles were stacked in bales twenty feet high and fresh ones in all sizes were presented in basket after basket. It was a chilehead's fantasy come true, and I couldn't resist. I picked up one of the vendor's red chiles, but before I could pop it in my mouth, she shook her head negatively and made a discouraging gesture with her hands. I just grinned at her and chewed up the chile without flinching, winning the admiration of the woman and the other nearby vendors, who, of course, had never heard of The Pope of Peppers.

Later, on a trip to Johore Baru, Malaysia, we found even more evidence of the intense love for chiles in this part of the world. In a supermarket in a shopping mall, there were two aisles fifty feet long that consisted of hundreds of brands of chile sauces stacked neatly on the shelves. Needless to say, we filled our basket with as many as we could—they were bound for Chip Hearn of Peppers.com, our friend who has the largest collection of hot sauces in the world!

In Singapore, I found more hot and spicy restaurants than bland ones! Chinese, Indian, Nonya, Malaysian, and Indonesian were the available options. My least favorite dish was sea slugs, which tasted like fishy gummy bears, and my favorite was the fish head curry—it doesn't sound very appetizing, but it was nothing short of spectacular—if you can get used to the fish staring at you.

In Japan, I judged the Japanese Scovie Awards, and was the honored guest. The spicy snacks were outstanding and quite hot, and I gave a little speech in front of several hundred guests, with a translator, of course. Like the rest of the world, Japan is heating up!

> In spite of regional differences, a unifying theme runs through Indonesia cooking: coconut and chile. The coconut palm is the most universal plant in the islands, and coconut milk and the grated meat pervade the cuisine. Indonesian cookery would be unthinkable without them. The use of coconut in cooking precedes that of the chile, which was introduced in the seventeenth century [some say the sixteenth]. When the chile arrived in Indonesia, it was welcomed enthusiastically and may now be considered an addiction.
>
> —Copeland Marks, author of 16 books on exotic cuisines

How to Ulek Sumatran Chiles

"Lovingly crushed, seeds and all, with a stone mortar called an *ulekan* and pestle (*ulek-ulek*), homemade Sumatran *sambal ulek* is what heats up the country's hottest cuisine. One expert on Indonesian cooking says if you're serious about it you'll always crush ingredients using a mortar and pestle. With Padang-style cuisine, I'd say this makes sense only if you crave exercise…The amount of processing that Sumatran dishes call for is best left to a food processor or blender. Otherwise, besides much tedious work, you actually risk burns to hands, eyes or whatever else the sambal touches." –Author Jeff Corydon

Meet the Enemy and Eat Him

"The use of chiles in cooking is limited, and as a result, Cambodian food is quite mild. However, says Cambodian Yann Ker, his countrymen are fond of using sliced chiles as a table condiment, and that is where the heat comes in. Mrs. Pheng Chu adds that one variety of Cambodian chile is so hot that its name, *mateh khamang*, means 'enemy.'"
—Alexandra Greeley

The Truth About Thai Heat

"For many *farangs*, Thai food is synonymous with the incendiary heat of chiles, and one of the most frequent comments about the cuisine is that it's very hot, if not at times too hot. Chalie is sensitive to this complaint and insists that well-prepared Thai dishes should be balanced, so that the spiciness of hot peppers is offset by the sweetness of coconut milk or palm sugar, the pungency of fresh herbs, the sourness of lime juice or tamarind, or the saltiness of *nam pla*.

Too often in Thai restaurants in the West that balance is out of whack. In traditional home-style cooking, Chalie explained, the mother spiced the dishes mildly and offered small bowls of hot sauce on the side so that each person could fire up his or her serving to taste. Only when she thought she didn't have enough food for a meal would the heat be increased to keep the family from eating too much." —Kemp M. Minifie, writing about the Thai Cooking School and its director, Chalie Amatyakul

Nothing Beats A Bug

At that moment we heard a friendly sizzle and smelled our favorite aromas: chile and garlic. We followed our noses to a food stall where a well-fed merchant smiled a greeting. Before him were two huge woks filled with dancing hot oil, one redolent of garlic, the other breathing ginger. Bowls of sliced garlic, crushed red chile, sliced green serranos and whole flaming-looking little orange peppers lay about. A large basket covered with a cloth mesh held the merchant's meat: giant locusts.

The merchant reached under the mesh and grabbed a large handful of the squirming giants and dropped them into the hot, garlic-scented oil. They sizzled and hissed and turned from green to golden brown. He put them in a bag and sprinkled them with soy sauce and crushed chile.

I broke the body into halves, gave Bruce one, and in unspoken agreement, we ate them simultaneously. No guts gushed.

"You know," Bruce said, "I've seen jumbo prawns smaller than these."

"Let's get the garlic flavor."

"With chile!"

"Yeah!"

"You know, these are like chips and salsa," I noted for the record.

"Or nachos."

Taking another one from the bag and sniffing its pungent garlicky-chile goodness, I said, "I wonder what they'll have for us at our next stop, in Burma."

A Wacky World Tour

Then we strolled about the bazaar, chatting with vendors, joking with children, and eating the food of Nero and John the Baptist.
—Richard Sterling, in Thailand at the Cholburi Provincial Bazaar

Thai Culinary Influences

What has long intrigued me about Thai food is its reflection of the unique way in which influences from neighboring countries have been adapted. As we tasted our way through five days of classes these culinary borrowings became clearer. From India came the curries, but, whereas Indian curries are based on spices, Thai curries are predominately herbal, with the prevailing flavors of coriander root, lemongrass, chiles, and basil and only the occasional use of cumin, coriander seed, and cardamom. Reminiscent of Chinese cuisine are the stir-fried meats and poultry and the noodle dishes, but the addition of such seasonings as shrimp paste, lime juice, tamarind, and basil makes them distant relations. The Thais adopted *sates*, the skewers of grilled meats served with a peanut sauce, from the Malaysians, but instead of a dry marinade the Thais often combine the spices with coconut milk and let the meat marinate in the mixture before grilling it." —Kemp M. Minifie, writing about the Thai Cooking School

Thai Food: Hurts So Good

"Real Thai food, unlike American versions of it, is one of the wonders of the world. I ate a take-out lunch in my kayak under the shade of a footbridge. I had roast chicken with a hot dipping sauce and an old favorite, *som tam*, a salad of unripe grated papayas in a marinade of lime juice, chile pepper, tamarind sauce, tiny dried shrimp, and peanuts. But I was no more used to the heat of the spices than I was to the heat of the sun. My mouth burned with a fire that teared my eyes. I remembered reading why this pepper pain became so habit

Small Thai chiles in the wholesale market, Bangkok, Thailand.
Photo courtesy of Sunbelt Archives

forming. The chile causes pain killers to be released by the brain, so eating the marinated shrimps became sort of a luncheon high."
–Chef and author Peter Aiken

How did Chile Peppers Get to China?
Some experts speculate that chiles were imported into China from Singapore, or carried inland from Macao, where hot dishes are more popular today than in neighboring Canton. It's more likely that chiles were introduced into the Sichuan region by sixteenth century Indian Buddhist missionaries traveling the "Silk Route" between India and China. After all, western Sichuan is closer to India than to either Macao or Singapore. No matter how they arrived in western China, chiles soon became enormously important to the food of the people.

Can You Cook Better Than an Asian Monkey?
Contrary to popular belief, chefs cooking in Sichuan or Hunan style are not trying to incinerate the people who eat their creations. Howard Hillman, an expert on world cuisines, has written of the way heat is applied in western China: "Even on the peasant level, the people prefer the dishes on the table to have degrees of hotness varying from mild to fiery. This is in contrast to the monotonous everything-as-hot-as-possible approach favored by many non-Chinese Sichuan restaurant- goers.

Making one Sichuan dish hotter than another is not a measure of a chef's talent; all it takes is the addition of extra chile, a feat that could be performed by a trained monkey. Epicures judge a Sichuan chef by the subtly complex overtones of his sauces and whether they complement the other ingredients in his dishes."

The Rooster Comes to America
Asian hot sauces are quite varied, from simple chile oils and sauces like the ubiquitous sriracha, to hot bean sauces to chile pastes—even commercial hoisin sauce has a little dried red chile in it. Chinese chile oil is made by simply steeping hot chiles in peanut oil; the oil then is used as a replacement for vegetable oils in salads and for frying. One of the most popular Asian hot sauces in the United States is Rooster Brand Sriracha Chili Sauce by Huy Fong Foods, which *Bon Apetit* Magazine named "condiment of the year" in 2010.

The sauce was developed by the company's founder, David Tran, an ethnic Chinese Vietnamese farmer who had grown chile peppers and sold chile sauce in Long Binh, a village just north of Saigon. He fled Vietnam in the late 1970s and arrived in the United States in 1980 as a part of the migration of the Vietnamese boat people following the Vietnam War. Its main ingredient is ripe jalapeño peppers.

The company is named for the old Taiwanese freighter that took Tran to Hong Kong in 1978 and its rooster logo comes from the fact that Tran was born in the Year of the Rooster. The bottles' trademark green top symbolizes the freshness of the chile used.

Is Sichuan Pepper Made From Chiles?

Sichuan peppers (known in Chinese as *hua jiao*) aren't related to chile peppers or black pepper. They're actually the fruits of the prickly ash tree (*Zanthoxylum piperitum*)! To make things more confusing, they've been marketed as "brown peppercorns," "Szechwan pepper," "Chinese pepper," "Japanese pepper," "aniseed pepper," "Spice pepper," "Chinese prickly-ash," "*Fagara*," "*sansho*," "Nepal pepper," "Indonesian lemon pepper," and others.

Sichuan peppers aren't exactly "hot" in the way white pepper or chile peppers can be. Instead, along with a citrusy flavor, the tiny fruits cause a numbing, tingling sensation in the mouth. The active ingredient in Sichuan peppers is *hydroxyl alpha sanshool* (or "sanshool" for short). So, while capsaicin causes spiciness in chile peppers, and piperidine causes the hot, biting flavor of black and white peppercorns, sanshool causes a "pins and needles" sensation, as if you've stuck a nine-volt battery on your tongue! The Chinese have a word for this; they call it *ma la*, which literally means "numbing" and "spicy."

Up until the sixteenth century, Sichuan peppers had been the primary "spicy" ingredient in Asian cuisine. This changed after Christopher Columbus introduced the chili pepper to the Old World. Hot chili peppers and peppercorns spread rapidly across Europe, the Middle East, and Asia, and suddenly, there was a new hot spice in town.

China Leads Chile Production, Lags in Manufacturing

The aggressive marketing of Chinese fresh and dried chile peppers has countries like Mexico and India trembling in their shoes, but there's one place where China is lagging far behind other pepper-loving countries. The first automated production line for chile sauce came online as recently as June of 2010. It was a project of Lameizi Food Stuff Co., Ltd., located in Hunan province.

Japanese Can't Take the Heat

Capsicums were introduced into Japan in the late 1500s or early 1600s and were used as a vegetable, spice, and ornamental plant. By the late 1800s, cultivation was extensive, and the Japanese varieties known as 'Santaka' and 'Hontaka' became famous for their high pungency. However, Japanese palates appear to be more attuned to milder peppers like bells. Japanese *shishito* peppers are becoming very popular among American gardeners and chile enthusiasts; they are prolific and easy to grow. An added bonus is the fact that these flavorful small chiles are fairly mild but have thinner walls than bells, making them suitable for flash-frying.

Bali Hot

"Balinese white rice forms the basis of all meals. The population of Bali is largely Hindu so there are no restrictions on eating pork or any other meats. However, meat dishes comprise only a small part of their diet. Western food is regarded as tasteless by the Balinese, who enjoy highly spiced and peppery dishes containing an abundance of onions, garlic, ginger, white-hot peppers, and fermented fish paste. Oddly, the nutmeg, cloves, and mace that give the "spice islands" their characteristic name are rarely used, although stretched cloths filled with drying cloves are a common sight in every small village. Coconut milk and ground peanuts impart a rich creaminess to sauces, whilst the rice, along with cucumber and banana taken as side dishes, cool the palate. –Writer Rosemary Ogilvie

Chapter 10 Chile Quiz: Asian Words for Chile Peppers

Match Column 1 with Column 2

1. **Tabia**   A. Chile peppers in Laotian.
2. **Cabe**   B. The Thai word for chile peppers.
3. **Sili**   C. Balinese word for chile peppers.
4. **Mak phet**   D. Burmese term for chiles.
5. **Prik**   E. Term for chile peppers in Indonesia and Malaysia.
6. **Nga yut thee** F. The Filipino (Tagalog) word for Capsicums.

Curries, with their vast partitioned platter
of curious condiments to lackey them, speak
for themselves. They sting like serpents,
stimulate like strychnine; they are subtle,
sensual like Chinese courtesans, sublime and
sacred, inscrutably inspiring and intelligently
illuminating, like Cambodian carvings.

—Aleister Crowley, British author,
occultist, and avid curry lover

Dave DeWitt's Chile Trivia

Chapter 11

Curious Curries and Indian Burns

I've eaten different kinds of curries in about eight different countries, so I can tell you that the title of my book *A World of Curries* is accurate.

Exploration, conquest, and constant collisions of cultures caused curries to spread far and wide from their native India. The worldwide trade in spices assisted greatly in the diffusion of curries because the basic curry spices became available in many lands, where they were combined with local spices and foodstuffs, thus transforming the nature of curries from locale to locale.

The story of the spread of curries around the world is also the story of Indian migration, and later emigration in the form of indentured servitude. The latter practice, called by historians "a new system of slavery," caused horrendous suffering among the Indian emigrants. However, it did spread Indian culture—and curries—to many parts of the globe.

Curry is everywhere these days. It is perhaps the favorite dish of Trinidad and Tobago. It is now the de facto National Dish of the United Kingdom, served in more than 7,000 curry restaurants. And curry has even spread to Germany as "curry-wurst," a street snack of sausages slathered with ketchup and sprinkled with chile powder and curry powder!

Back in India, things are only getting hotter, as the 'Bhut Jolokia' pepper got the country enormous publicity despite the fact that the origin of that variety is Trinidad. India is still one of the hottest countries in the world in terms of its various spicy cuisines, you know there's going to be some chile-oriented weird stuff happening there!

Pat Chapman, England's "King of Curries," took my wife and I on a culinary tour of India that focused on the chefs to the Taj Hotel group, and the food was spectacular even if the country is the strangest—and most fascinating—place I've ever visited. To hell with the Taj Mahal in the grubby city of Agra, I much more enjoyed sitting in the back room of a carpet shop in Udaipur while the owner fixed us the very hot Jungli Mans with just a gas flame, a pot, some chicken, oil and red chile. It was simple but amazing, and we washed it down with shots of Indian vodka. Now *that's* India.

> There are...hundreds of curries; curries of meat, fish, prawns, lobsters; bamboo curries and curried fruits; and mixed curries. Curries are not only eaten in India and Pakistan, but in every country where spices are cheap and plentiful.
> —Harvey Day, author of *The Curries of India*

> There is reason to assume that the ambrosia of which the ancient poets spoke of so often was a kind of ginger chile called pinang curry...
> —C.L. Leipoldt, the Afrikaans poet and gourmet

What Does The Word "Curry" Mean?

The Oxford English Dictionary defines curry as: "A preparation of meat, fish, fruit, or vegetables, cooked with a quantity of bruised spices and turmeric, and used as a relish or flavouring, especially for dishes composed of or served with rice." A secondary definition says that curry powder may be used in the cooking process.

The term "curry" reflects the evolution of language, and the need to designate, in English, dishes that were based on various spice mixtures. Indeed, "curry" has come to mean, in English, different spice mixtures that are used in a similar manner in countries throughout the world. "Curry," explains Yohanni Jones, author of *Dishes from Indonesia*, "is a word frequently used by foreigners to describe Indonesian dishes cooked with coconut milk." Santha Rama Rau, author of the *Time-Life* book on Indian cooking, says that the "proper sense" of the word 'curry' is "a highly seasoned stew with plenty of sauce."

Indian food expert Julie Sahni notes that the word *kari* is a shortened version of *kari-pulia*, or kari leaves, meaning the leaves of the curry plant, *Murraya koenigii*, a common ingredient in Indian curry blends.

The word has even crept into slang, as in the American and British phrase "currying favor" (which originally meant "to please with cookery") and the Australian "to give curry," which means to abuse or rebuke someone.

Was "Curry" Actually Coined by An Irishman?

Perhaps the most unusual theory of the origin of the word "curry" comes from Selat Elbis Sopmi of London's Punjab Restaurant, who wrote in *The Curry Club Magazine* that some centuries ago an Irish sea captain married into a wealthy family. The captain's gambling led to the demise of the family, which kept a large stable of racehorses. They were forced to sell the best of the horses and eat the rest. The Irishman used the word *cuirreach*, Irish for racetrack, and told everyone he had been reduced to eating *cuirreach gosht*, or racetrack meat. "Over the ages, this has become, through usage," claims Sopmi, "the word as we know it, curry." I'm not sure I buy this, but it's a great story.

Dave DeWitt in turban as he prepares for his first camel ride. 1996 photo by Mary Jane Wilan

A Wacky World Tour

How Long Has Curry Been Around?

Curry-like spice mixtures date back to at least 4,000 B.C. In excavations of the ancient cities of Harpatta and Mohenjo-Daro in the Indus Valley in what is now Pakistan, grinding stones were found that contained traces of mustard seed, cumin, saffron, fennel, and tamarind. Since all of these spices appear in curries, it is not unreasonable to assume that the ancient Indus Valley people were cooking with curry spices 6,000 years ago—although no recipes survive.

The King of Curries

Curry reigns supreme in the United Kingdom, as witnessed by: a curry magazine, a curry club with 13,000 members, nine curry cookbooks in print, dozens of curry products, thousands of curry restaurants, and even a detailed guide to all those restaurants. The king of this spiced-up madness is Pat Chapman from Surrey, who started The Curry Club in 1982.

"I was weaned on curries," he said. "When I was very, very young in the early '50s, my parents used to take me to one of the six Indian restaurants in the entire country. Now there are more than 7,000, with 1,500 in London alone. There are more curry houses in the U.K. than in all of India!"

To what does Pat attribute this intense interest in hot and spicy curries in an otherwise bland England? "There were two waves of interest," he explained. "One after the end of the British Raj in India, when the soldiers returned. The other happened much later, starting in the 1950's and '60s, when Indian immigration was at its peak."

Is Curry a Spice?

This fiction continues to spread despite numerous books on spices and Indian cooking. Curry leaf (*Murraya koenigii*) is a single herb used in some curries, but in reality, there are dozens and dozens of herbs, spices, fruits, rhizomes, bulbs, pulses, nuts, and other ingredients which are combined to make curries.

While curry leaf is used in some curries, not all curries contain curry leaf. Confused yet?

Talk About a Hot Curry!

A British Airways flight attendant caused a near panic on a flight from Heathrow Airport to Miami when she used the plane's microwave to heat up a take-out curry meal and the curry exploded, causing the microwave to catch on fire. The flight attendant staff had to use a fire extinguisher to control the flames. A spokesman for the airline said: "A member of the crew incorrectly used one of the on-board microwaves to heat a meal which resulted in a small fire within the oven itself. As a precaution, a specialist extinguisher was used on the microwave, however at no time was there any danger to passengers or the aircraft." If that is true, the question remains: why did the incident result in $40,000 worth of damage to the aircraft? British Airways has now banned cabin crews from using the microwaves to heat up their own food, and sent a memo to staff noting that the airline microwaves are twice as powerful as the home units.

What? No Servants to Grind Your Masala?

In India, as Tom Stobart, author of *The Cook's Encyclopedia*, observes: "Books commonly say that Indians do not use curry powder. This may have been true in the days when even the servants had servants and the *masala* of fresh ginger, garlic, onion, coconut, green chile, and spices was ground on the stone freshly for each dish. But today, a First World cost of servants has caught up with Third World households, and ready-ground spice mixtures are no longer beyond the pale."

This is not to say that Indian cooks now use commercial preparations to the exclusion of homemade curries, but rather that they have now the option because of the vast number of commercial products on the market.

Is Curry Powder The "Big Mac" of Spice Blends?

Juel Anderson, author of *The Curry Primer*, has pointed out: "Through time, commercial spice mixtures have become so uniform a blend that most of us know curries only as yellow-colored foods with a standard aroma, often peppery-hot and as predictable in flavor as a Big Mac."

Indeed, there is a sameness to commercial curry powders, especially those made in the United States to the 1977 USDA standards for curry powder, which calls for the following percentages of spices: coriander, 36; turmeric, 28; cumin, 10; fenugreek, 10; white pepper, 5; allspice, 4; mustard, 3; red pepper, 2; and ginger, 2.

However, I should point out that there are many imported curry powders, especially from India, which vary in flavor considerably because they contain a wider variety of spices used in many different percentages. Maybe I'll sprinkle some on my next Happy Meal.

A Wacky World Tour

Creepy Crowley Crazy for Curry

"Curries, with their vast partitioned platter of curious condiments to lackey them, speak for themselves. They sting like serpents, stimulate like strychnine; they are subtle, sensual like Chinese courtesans, sublime and sacred, inscrutably inspiring and intelligently illuminating, like Cambodian carvings." —Aleister Crowley, British author, occultist, and avid curry lover

Known by many as "The Beast," the mystic Aleister Crowley died on December 1, 1947, at the age of 72. His final request was for his friends to gather a year after his death and remember him with a dinner of his favorite food, curry. And so Gerald Yorke, Frieda Lady Harris, Louis Wilkinson, and others ate at an Indian restaurant and retired to Yorke's place for an evening of reminiscing. This recipe was taken directly from Aleister's papers in the Crowley Archives at Bird Library, Syracuse University. No specific amounts were given for many ingredients, so add those to suit your personal taste. This dish is reported to be diabolically tasty.

Riz Aleister Crowley

(To be eaten with curry.)

> 1 cup brown basmati rice
> Sea salt
> 1/4 cup sultanas
> 1/4 cup slivered almonds
> 1/4 cup pistachio nuts
> powdered clove
> powdered cardamom
> turmeric powder (enough to colour the rice to a clear golden tint)
> 2 tablespoons butter

Bring two cups of salted water to a bowl. Throw in the rice, stirring regularly.

Test the rice after about ten minutes "by taking a grain, and pressing between finger and thumb. It must be easily crushed, but not sodden or sloppy. Test again, if not right, every two minutes."

When ready, pour cold water into the saucepan.

Empty the rice into a colander, and rinse under cold tap.

Put colander on a rack above the flames, if you have a gas stove, and let it dry. If, like me, your stove is electric, the rice can be dried by placing large sheets of paper towel over and under the rice, soaking up the water. Preferably the rice should seem very loose, almost as if it it has not been cooked at all. When you've removed as much water as you can, remove the paper towel.

Place the rice back into the pot on a much lower temperature.

Stirring continuously, add the butter, sultanas, almonds, pistachio nuts, a dash or two of cloves and a dash of cardamom.

Add enough turmeric that the rice, after stirring, is "uniform, a clear golden colour, with the green pistachio nuts making it a Poem of Spring."

What's In Curry Powder?

Indian food expert Julie Sahni takes a liberal view of the most basic ingredients required to make a curry: "For a spice blend to be called a curry powder, the mixture must contain three core spices: coriander, turmeric, and pepper." Others will disagree, asking, "where's the cumin?" or any other of their favorite spices. The point here is that many spice blends not originally defined as curry powders, such as those from North Africa and the Middle East, can fit into the broad category of curries.

Are Indian Spices Safe?

Unfortunately, not always. Pesticide residues in Indian chile peppers are high, due to the lack of national standards and oversight in agricultural and manufacturing practices across the country. In 2005 Indian chile imports were banned from the U.K. following the recall of 15 million tons of food made with Indian chile powder that was contaminated by a highly carcinogenic colorant known as Sudan-1.

Spices in the Mapusa Market, Goa, India. Photo courtesy of Sunbelt Archives

A Wacky World Tour

The dye is normally used in shoe polish, coloring solvents, oils, waxes and gasoline. It has been shown to cause cancer in mice and in tests on human liver cells.

Other issues plaguing the Indian spice industry include elevated levels of lead in chile powder and other products. Aflatoxin, another highly carcinogenic material, has been found in unacceptable levels in dried chile products. Aflatoxin is produced by the Aspergillus fungus and invades the pods while they are drying. The best way to protect yourself against spice contamination is to buy organic spices

Can I Make An Authentic Curry Outside of India?
The answer is a resounding yes. Virtually every exotic curry ingredient is available in the United States in Asian markets or by mail order. Besides, across the Indian subcontinent, as well as in other curry countries, cooks boldly experiment, and it is possible to get five or six variations for the same recipe. So, cooks should just use curry recipes as a rough guide, and feel free to experiment.

Is 'Bhut Jolokia' Native to India?
No it's not. The story of how this superhot variety came to India is described in detail in chapter 13, Superhot Stuff. Since 'Bhut' peppers are part of the *Capsicum chinense* family, they are native to the Caribbean, specifically Trinidad.

'Bhut Jolokia' chile pods, fresh (left) and dried (right). Despite their Indian-sounding name, these chiles hail from the Caribbean. Photo by Harald Zoschke

Is This Indian Lady Immune to the Heat of Chiles?
You be the judge: in 2009, Anandita Dutta Tamuly, a 25-year-old mother from Assam, consumed 60 fiery 'Bhut Jolokia' peppers in two minutes on television in India. Before devouring the peppers, she smeared seeds on her eyelids with no apparent ill effect. There was a rumor that she had set a Guinness World Record, but there was no official entry and Guinness rejected the claim. But there are pictures to prove that Tamuli did

indeed polish off a pile of pepper pods—with pepper seeds on her eyelids. Ouch! Some people are born without capsaicin receptors, and obviously she's one of them.

Is Guntur, India, the Chile Capital of the Entire World?

Journalist Anthony Spaeth traveled to India to check out this claim. "In Guntur," he wrote, "salted chiles are eaten for breakfast. Snacks are batter-fried chiles with chile sauce. The town's culinary pride are fruits and vegetables preserved in oil and chile, particularly its *karapo* pickles: red chiles pickled in chile."

Legend and lore about chiles figure prominently in the culture of Guntur. The people often dream about them, and they believe that hot tempers arise from heavy chile eating and that chiles increase sexual desire. Children begin to eat chile at age five and quickly build up an incredible tolerance.

"Chile is so ingrained in the culture of Guntur that an event like a chile-eating contest would be a silly redundancy," observed Spaeth.

India's Super Chilehead Baby

A 17-month-old toddler from Assam happily devours locally grown superhot peppers. His parents say that he "gleefully munches a handful of 'Bhut Jolokia' with batting an eyelid." He recently ate about 50 of the peppers in about four hours without showing any signs of tears or burning sensation. The child reportedly became hooked on the peppers when he was just about eight months old. "I was cooking in my kitchen and he was crawling on the floor when he laid his hands on some chillies and ate them. I cried for help but the kid was fine," his mother said.

Chapter 11 Quiz: Curry Countries

Match the name of the curry in Column 1 with the kocation in Column 2.

1. **Rendang**	**A.** Sri Lanka
2. **Mulligatawny**	**B.** Malaysia
3. **Gaeng Pannang Nua**	**C.** Thailand
4. **Sindhi Gosht**	**D.** England
5. **Meenu Kootu**	**E.** Trinidad
6. **Bairather Sepiyan**	**F.** South India
7. **Gaeng Mussaman**	**G.** Martinique
8. **Curried Chicken and Roti**	**H.** Indonesia
9. **Vindaloo**	**I.** Myanmar
10. **Pork Colombo**	**J.** Pakistan

A Wacky World Tour

Part IV

The Outer Limits of Heat

The fact that capsaicin causes pain to mammals seems to be accidental. Birds, which also eat fruits, don't have the same biochemical pain pathway, so they don't suffer at all from capsaicin. But in mammals it stimulates the very same pain receptors that respond to actual heat. Chili pungency is not technically a taste; it is the sensation of burning, mediated by the same mechanism that would let you know that someone had set your tongue on fire.

—Science writer James Gorman

Dave DeWitt's Chile Trivia

Chapter 12

Blazing Animal Encounters

Birds love chile peppers because, lacking lips with capsaicin receptors, they cannot feel the heat that mammals do. Birds were spreading the tiny wild chiltepins before mankind even appeared in the New World, and they get a lot of vitamin A from the pods, which improves the color of their plumage. So in the early days of *Chile Pepper* magazine, we spent a lot of time answering this important question from our readers: Will putting chile peppers in my wild bird seed in the feeder deter those *#*@&^ squirrels? And we had similar questions about repelling rabbits in the garden, deer in back yards eating flowers and vegetables, and mice in the basement.

The answer? Yes and no. First, for squirrels, it's best to use very hot chile powder because it mixes very well with the seed and cannot be removed by either the birds or those pesky squirrels. Except when it rains, and then you have a mess on your hands. And unless you do what the Africans do to repel elephants—building chile hedges and creating capsaicin bombs to drive them off—chiles will not repel deer. Mice have been known to eat dried chile pods, so it's not going to work for them.

Most pets don't like chile peppers and avoid them once they've tasted one. However, my wife and I had a tabby cat named Bombette, who would dip her paw in red chile sauce cooking on the stove and lick it off. All of this tells me that mammals are like humans and their tolerance varies considerably depending on the number of capsaicin receptors they inherited from their parents.

Hot Sauce and Salsa Names with Animal Themes

Red Rooster Hot Sauce
Coyote Cafe Howlin' Hot Sauce
African Rhino Peri-peri Hot Sauce
Gator Hammock
Frog Ranch Tadpole Salsa
Bullfrog Salsa
Viper Venom
Snakebite
Bat's Brew
Iguana Red Pepper Sauce
Mad Dog Liquid Fire
Mustang Salsa
Hogs Breath Salsa
Virgin Fire Dragon's Breath Red
Ass Kickin' Hot Sauce
Baboon Ass Gone Rabid
Bee Sting Pepper Sauce
Fire Ant Juice
Great White Shark Predator Hot Sauce
Hog's Ass Hot Sauce
Lizard Spit Habanero Sauce
Rudolph the Red-Assed Reindeer Cayenne Hot Sauce

Good Thing it Wasn't a Ristra of Peter Peppers

As reported in *The New York Times*, a mother and her daughter were shopping in a store in Great Barrington, Massachusetts that sells Southwestern apparel and memorabilia.

"What's that, Mommy?" the small child asks, pointing to a ristra of red chiles.

"I don't know dear," her mother replies. "I think it's part of a dead cow."

See Ya Later, Gourmet Meat of the '90s

"Hello, my name is Byron and I'll be your waiter tonight. Our special is a tender Sauteed Fillet of Lagarto in a Chipotle Aioli Sauce."

"And what, pray tell, is a Lagarto?" asked the customer at the chic new restaurant, Al Dente's.

"It's a white meat, very lean yet succulent, with faint flavor overtones of poultry. Farm-raised, of course."

"Of course, but what is this creature? Some kind of ostrich?"

"Not exactly."

"A fish like tilapia?"

"Larger."

"Kangaroo?"

Byron the waiter stood tall and looked the customer straight in the eye. "It's alligator, sir. The finest hand-fed, farm-raised, low-fat, high-protein, low-calorie alligator meat from Jacques' Crocs and Farm Pride Processors in Scott, Louisiana."

"You expect me to eat a large lizard?"

"Have you eaten frog's legs?"

"Sure."

"Then you've eaten swamp-dwelling amphibians. How about raw oysters?"

"Yes."

"Those are bottom-scavenging mollusks. Vermicelli?"

"Well...."

"That's Italian for 'little worms.' And you're worried about alligator, traditional food of the Seminoles for increasing male potency?"

"I'll have a large Fillet of Lagarto, cooked medium."

"Good choice. May I suggest a Savignon Blanc to accompany your Lagarto?"

African Elephants Not Fond of Peppers

Lions aren't the only African fauna deterred by the powerful pod. Elephants, capable of massive destruction in agricultural areas, can be driven off by the smoke from "dung bombs," briquettes made from crushed chile peppers and animal poo. According to Loki Osborn of the Elephant Pepper Development Trust, planting rows of pepper plants around fields creates a barrier that elephants are reluctant to cross, as does slathering chile-infused grease on fences. "In areas where farmers are using our community-based problem-animal control techniques, most farmers have reduced crop loss by at least 90 percent," Osborn said. Today about 600,000 elephants roam Africa, with the largest populations found in the southern, eastern, and central areas of the continent.

Talk About Asking for a Kick in the Head!

A horse trainer at Gulfstream Park racetrack in Florida was accused of rubbing Fiery Jack cayenne pepper ointment on the genitals of horses to make them run faster...Frank Passero denied it, saying that he just rubbed it on the leg muscles.

Does This Mean Rats are Smarter than Chileheads?

Chile is a substance that most mammals will avoid as they would a poison. In contrast, birds and reptiles seem to be unaffected by its heat properties. Through a series of studies, psychologist Paul Rozin, Ph.D. found that it is practically impossible to induce a preference for chile peppers in rats, and subsequent experiments with dogs and chimpanzees have had limited success. A study he conducted in 1979 states that humans are the only mammals that "reverse their natural rejection" to bitter, "innately unpalatable substances" such as nicotine, coffee, alcohol, tobacco...and chile peppers. In fact, they can learn to prefer the flavor and physiological effects of these ingredients to the point of choosing to eat them regularly.

A Fiery Fish Story

After Gary Waters of Douglasville, Georgia, poured some of his home-made Chef's Boy Hidy Original Triple-X Habanero Sauce on a cigar minnow and trolled it right next to the beach in Panama City, Florida, he hooked and boated a 72-pound wahoo that was more than six feet long.

Capsaicin May Prevent Salmonella In Poultry

Researchers at Virginia Tech have had good results in increasing Salmonella resistance in poultry by adding capsaicin to their feed, according to Audrey McElroy, assistant professor of poultry science. The laboratory theorized that a diet that included some form of hot peppers might protect broilers and other commercial poultry from intestinal disease. The research began with the purchase of 1,530 commercial meat chicks, dividing them into three groups, and feeding each group a standard corn and soybean meal-based diet for 42 days. McElroy fed the plain feed to the first group, but added five parts per million of pure capsaicin to the feed of the second group, and 20 parts per million to the third group's feed. She then infected the chicks with Salmonella enteritidis at 21, 28, and 42 days of age. She discovered that both the low and the high level of capsaicin increased resistance to the Salmonella without adversely affecting food consumption, weight gain, or the taste of the chicken when cooked.

The poultry that McElroy utilized seem to have no problem with the taste or sting of the capsaicin. "If we can prove that feeding capsaicin to birds does reduce Salmonella in a commercial poultry-production situation, it would provide a non-antibiotic way of reducing food-borne pathogens," she says. "Consumers want an antibiotic-free product, and this may provide the answer."

Chile-Addicted Deer Sentenced to Death

New Mexico Game and Fish Department officials sentenced five chile-head mule deer to die by firing squad for eating nearly two acres of chile peppers and severely damaging three additional acres. The depredations occurred on the farm of Ben Bouvet in Arrey, just north of Hatch.

Department officers attempted to scare the deer from the field for about a month, but the chile-starved creatures could not control their urges. The names of those benefiting from the pre-marinated venison were not made public. No attempt was made to find a "halfway pasture" for the addicted deer.

Tabasco® Outfoxes Foxes

Scientists taking ground-temperature measurements at Prudhoe Bay, Alaska, were troubled by foxes chewing through their instrumentation cables. According to Dr. Frederick Nelson, who led the project, the scientists wanted to protect their cables without killing or harming the foxes, but could not come up with a method until a curious coincidence occurred.

Dr. Nelson, writing in the journal *Nature*, noticed that hot pepper sauces were abundant in the oil field dining rooms because many of the oil workers were from the Gulf Coast and east Texas. That fact gave him an idea. "Replacement cables were coated with Tabasco® pepper sauce," he wrote. "A layer of clear silicone sealant was applied with a caulking gun, distributed evenly with a sauce-saturated cloth, and allowed to dry. While the sealant was slightly tacky, pepper sauce was applied liberally to its surface."

The result? "There was no further damage to our instrumentation in two field seasons," Dr. Nelson reported. "No toothmarks penetrated the cables, which demonstrates the effectiveness and tenacity of the pungency of pepper sauce."

Chile Peppers Deter Elephants

In southern Africa's Mid-Zambezi Valley, peaceful coexistence between farmers and wild animals can be a bit complicated. Over the last two decades, so many people have moved into the area that elephants, among other animals, are forced to roam and search for food, and crops are often destroyed. The traditional methods of driving elephants away, such as with fire or hunting, negatively impact the elephant population, plus they do not prevent future raids. Instead, the Elephant Pepper Development Trust, with a grant from the World Bank's Development Marketplace, taught farmers to cultivate chiles, which serve as a natural defense against elephant intrusions. Farmers can create an ecologically friendly barrier by rubbing chile oil on fences—and chiles can be a very lucrative crop.

Spicy Spray Is Best Grizzly Repellent

Imagine this scenario: you are preparing a stew with dried green chiles at your campsite in Yellowstone National Park when a gigantic silver-tipped grizzly bear blunders into the camp and suddenly charges you. What do you do? Reach for your rifle? No, rifles are illegal in National Parks. You throw the chile stew in the bear's face, of course, because you realize that the capsaicin in the chiles will repel the bear.

Sound a bit far-fetched? Not according to scientists at the University of Montana, who began testing hot pepper sprays in 1981 as grizzly repellents. During the studies, a number of capsaicin-based sprays were used on caged grizzlies and black bears that were provoked into charging and then blasted with liquified hot peppers. The results were encouraging: "The bears stopped in a flash," wrote one witness, "began rubbing their eyes and noses—a grizzly's sense of smell is among the keenest of any mammal's—and retreated."

Based on the Montana research, a Florida manufacturer developed a spray called "Animal Repel," which atomizes an oleoresin capsicum and shoots it 10 to 15 feet in a tightly focused mist. During an unplanned test in the Arctic, a biologist confronted by an ill-tempered polar bear sprayed it with a shot of Animal Repel and the bear ran off in tears. Of course, since bears are unpredictable and often break off their attacks for no reason at all, Animal Repel is no guarantee of survival. And if you're going to resort to tossing chile stew at a charging bear, better make sure you're cooking with 'Bhut Jolokia' pods.

Capsicum Spray Routs Grizzly Bear, Saves Two Lives

"It's horrible to be eaten alive by an animal," said a man who credits a Capsicum spray with saving his life. Mark Matheny, a general contractor from Bozeman, Montana, and his partner, Dr. Fred Bahnson, were bow hunting for elk in the forest. They surprised a female grizzly and her three cubs feasting on a freshly-killed elk and the grizzly mama instantly reacted to protect her cubs.

"She charged with incredible speed," said Matheny. "I had no time to do anything. I held my bow up in front of me for protection, and she just knocked it out of my hand."

The grizzly smashed Matheny to the ground and seized his head in her jaws. Meanwhile, Bahnson had drawn his can of ten percent capsicum oleoresin spray and charged the bear, screaming at the top of his lungs. The bear turned and was hit directly in the eyes with the caustic spray.

Seemingly oblivious, the grizzly then knocked Bahnson to the ground, turned back to Matheny, and mauled him again. Bahnson re-

The Outer Limits of Heat

covered and charged the bear again, pointing the can of Capsicum spray at it. He pressed the valve. The can was empty.

The grizzly knocked Bahnson down again, bit him on the arm, and was about to rip out his throat when the spray finally took effect and the bear suddenly broke off the attack, ran back to her cubs and then tore off into the woods.

Matheny suffered from sixteen inches of bear bites on his face and head, which required more than 100 stitches to close. But he survived, thanks to his partner Dr. Bahnson, who just happens to specialize in facial reconstruction. And thanks to a certain capsicum spray, whose brand name remains unknown.

Cows Crave Chile Byproducts

Researchers at New Mexico State University in Las Cruces, led by Dr. Clint Löest of the Department of Animal and Range Sciences, are exploring the possibilities of utilizing the 15,000 tons of chile byproduct (pods, skins, stems, and leaves) that are generated by growers and processors each year as cattle feed, particularly for dairy cattle. Research conducted by University scientists demonstrated that feeding dairy cattle an alfalfa-based diet including 20 percent chile byproducts (mostly pods and skins) did not have any large negative effects on milk constituents and appeared to increase total milk production.

Interestingly, cattle not only will tolerate chile pods and byproducts, they actually seem to want them. Dairy ranchers report cows rushing from all over the pens to feed on the chile byproducts when they are pitched into the feedlots. Such a love of chile contradicts conventional wisdom that holds that capsaicin evolved to repel mammals. The cattle are not fazed by the heat of the pod waste, giving rise to a new ranching expression: a "chile-head of cattle."

Barnacles Can't Take the Heat

Just when you thought you had heard of every possible use for capsaicin, along comes Ken Fisher and his Barnacle Ban. This Pittsburgh inventor has received a patent for his formula for mixing epoxy paint and capsicum oleoresin to form a paint that is hated by the mollusks of the world—namely, barnacles, zebra mussels, and tubeworms, which will not attach themselves to surfaces of ships and intake valves coated with Barnacle Ban.

The U.S. Navy is now testing Barnacle Ban, which reputedly lasts three or four times longer than the Navy's eighteen-month protection from copper anti-fouling paint—and is much cheaper. Fisher explained how his concoction works: "When barnacles or zebra mussels get on it, they get right off because it attacks the nervous system and sends pain messages." Sore mussels? I guess.

Hot Peppers Are Definitely For the Birds

Did capsaicin evolve to protect chile peppers from mammalian predators? That's the theory of Dr. Michael Nee of the New York Botanical Garden. Scientists have long speculated that plants produce secondary metabolites, chemicals that are not required for the primary life support of the plant. These metabolites fight off animal predators and perhaps even competing plant species.

In the journal *HerbalGram*, Nee speculates that the capsaicin in chiles may be such a metabolite. It prevents animals from eating the chiles so that they can be consumed by fruit-eating birds that prefer red fruits with small seeds. Mammals perceive a burning sensation from capsaicin but birds do not. The seeds pass through the birds' digestive tracts intact and encased in a perfect natural fertilizer. Experts believe that the wild chiltepin (*C. annuum var. aviculare*) was spread by this method from South America to what is now the U.S.-Mexico border.

A Squirrely Solution

One of the most perplexing problems facing suburbanites these days is keeping squirrels out of their bird feeders. Numerous feeders have been invented that are supposedly squirrel-proof, but the clever squirrels defeat them all. Even a book has been written on the subject!

But now a Maryland company is marketing a product called "Squirrel-Away," which repels the rodents. "Squirrels will fly off the feeder," says their literature, "shaking their heads in disbelief as they head for the nearest bird bath."

The "mystery ingredient" in Squirrel-Away happens to be habanero chile powder, which is mixed with the bird seed. Actually, any hot chile powder will work—until the squirrels become chileheads, that is!

As an interesting sidebar to this story, a recent report from the Netherlands tells of Tabasco® sauce being mixed with water (one part to 600) and sprayed on crops as a pigeon repellent. Question: were the pigeons repelled by the capsaicin, or by the vinegar?

I like the excitement...the raw adrenal energy...
a kind of hormonal buzz.

—James Beard Award winner
Robert Del Grande

Dave DeWitt's Chile Trivia

Chapter 13

The Passionate Pepper

Chile peppers had an intense effect on one of our writers, Bob Slents-Kesler, who wrote *Romancing the Sauce*: "At first it was sweet. It teased me, as if to make me want more—as if to make me believe it would never hurt me. And then the truth came out. A flood of saliva gushed from every gland inside my mouth. Philippe stepped back. My jaw dropped open, and I gagged. How can I describe this feeling, when words don't work? Dave's Insanity Sauce seemed to be doing two things at once: sledge-hammering a metal spike through my mouth to the back of my throat, while repeatedly kicking me in the stomach with steel-toed boots. The floodgates of my nostrils burst open. Tears rushed from my eyes and poured down my face. I could barely stand the pain, even as my brain screamed in ecstasy: Yes, yes, yes. Harder. Faster. Burn me. Humiliate me." Poor Bob—he's still addicted.

Chiles and sex are associated together in at least two popular movies. In *Woman on Top*, the lovely Spanish actress Penelope Cruz is Isabelle, a young Brazilian woman who escapes her hometown and gets a cooking show in San Francisco, stunning all the men with her ways to cook with chiles. The equally beautiful Juliette Binoche portrays a peripatetic single mother in *Chocolat*, who arrives in a sleepy French village and establishes a chocolate shop during Lent. The action is built around a mysterious chocolate specialty spiced up with chile—her secret ingredient.

And what could be funnier—or sexier—than the Chili Pepper Vibrator, sold by many online and brick-and-mortar sex shops in the

United States? And I must not overlook the Chile Peppers Spicy Sex Collection, which is a vibrator with three chile pod-shaped sleeves in red, yellow, and green. And Adam and Eve, an online sex shop sells: "Muy Caliente! The Perfect Recipe For Red-Hot SEX! 3 Savory Chile Pepper Stimulators!"

The world of chiles is drenched in sex. Just conjure up the image of the 'Peter Pepper'!

> A husband can tell how much his wife loves him by how much hot pepper is in his food. If it is bland to his taste, she doesn't love him any more and he is very hurt. She must use the hot spice with a heavy hand to assure him of her devotion.
>
> —Bea Sandler, author of *The African Cookbook*

Do Chiles Make Women Irresistible?

A quick study of world cultures will show a basic belief that chiles will improve the attractiveness of women. Before Henry Stanley tracked down David Livingstone, the good doctor had noticed that West African women bathed in water to which ground red pepper—he called it paprika—had been added because they believed it would make them more beautiful. The origin and effectiveness of the chile bath are obscure, however. Mayan women also used chile as a beauty aid, specifically for skin care. However, their technique left a lot to be desired. The women washed their skin with hot urine, applied chile powder, and then repeated the procedure. I guess being willing to play around with hot urine might make you attractive to some guys, but seriously, do you really want to go there?

Do Men Eat Spicy Food to Impress Women?

Here's the true test of devotion: does your guy love you enough to eat a 'Bhut Jolokia'? A study in England revealed that men exaggerate the amount of spicy foods they can consume in order to impress their dates and mates. And when alcohol is thrown into the mix, the men exaggerate even more (go figure). News correspondent Roger Kaplinsky-Dwarika visited curry houses in the Hammersmith area of London and quoted a 22-year-old partier named Jon, who said it was a "lad thing" to have a few drinks and then "go off for a steaming curry—the hotter the better." His friend Ken agreed: "A guy has to be seen to show off to his friends, and if he can't do that with an expensive car or a nice house, then the thing to do, it seems, is to eat the hottest chiles in front of his friends." The theory of Richard Wiseman, a senior psychologist at the University of Hertsfordshire, is that such behavior has to do with our evolutionary past. "Males who exhibited the the greatest ability to withstand pain stood a better chance of attracting more females," he said.

Is Chile an Aphrodisiac?

The chile pepper was late in arriving in India, but its effect was even more powerful than black pepper, which was a hot food that held a significant place in Indian legend and lore. The *Kama Sutra* reported: "If a man, after anointing his *lingam* with a mixture of the powders of the white thorn apple, the long pepper and the black pepper, and honey, engages in sexual union with a woman, he makes her subject to his will." Don't try this at home.

So it is not surprising that many books on the subject of aphrodisiacs list both black pepper and chile pepper prominently. In *Plants of Love*, by Christian Ratsch, *Capsicum annuum* is listed just after *Cannabis sativa*, and the text states: "The cayenne pepper is considered a hot food that heatens the sexual drive.... When used as an aphrodisiac, great care should be taken to avoid overdosage." It should be noted that the primary use of chiles as an aphrodisiac is internal; that is, they are eaten, not rubbed on the genitalia.

Menu for a Hot Aphrodisiacal Tryst

Chiles have long been considered to be aphrodisiacs, according to H.E, Wedeck in his *Dictionary of Aphrodisiacs*. In his listing for paprika, for example, he writes: "This condiment is credited with decided erotic impulses." Additionally, he lists dozens and

The Outer Limits of Heat

dozens of other foods that are credited with stimulating the libido, so it makes sense that if these foods were spiced up, they'd be a sort of culinary Viagra. Here, then, are our Recipes for Romance.

Cocktails: Dry martinis made with Absolut Peppar or Stolichnaya Pertsovka vodka.

Appetizers: Raw oysters with habanero hot sauce; caviar sprinkled with a mild hot sauce.

Soup: French onion soup with ancho chile.

Salad: Radish, rocket, shallots, poblano chile, artichoke hearts, and tomato (love-apple) salad with a dressing of oil, vinegar, garlic, and black pepper.

Wine: Any good, dry white wine.

Main Dish: Chicken Paprikash.

Side dish: Green peas boiled with onions and spiced with cayenne, cinnamon, ginger, and cardamom (from *The Perfumed Garden*, the 16th century Arabian sex manual).

Side Dish: Garlic Mashed Potatoes with Pimentón, the Spanish smoked paprika and ghee, Indian clarified butter.

Desserts: Rice mixed with honey of equal weight (from the *Ananga-Ranga*, an ancient Hindu sex manual), served with grapes and chocolate candies.

Dessert Wine: Disaster Bay Chilli Wine from Australia (fermented from six different varieties of chiles, no grapes).

It's a bird, it's a plane, it's a chile vibrator!

Aphrodisiac Haggis for the Royal Couple

When Prince Charles married Camilla, Duchess of Cornwall, one of the most unique wedding gifts came from a Scotland-based German sausage-maker named Stefan Gellrich. The proprietor of "BuckieHam Palace" sent Charles and his bride a wedding hamper full of royal morsels, including a specially-seasoned aphrodisiac haggis. Stefan used hot Cajun spices with erotic fruits such as apricots, figs and pine nuts, to create a hot-blooded feeling.

In case the exact ingredients of haggis have slipped your mind, it's a dish containing sheep's heart, liver, and lungs, minced with onion, oatmeal, suet, spices, and salt, which is then combined and simmered inside the sheep's stomach for 3 hours. It's considered to be the national dish of Scotland, poor wee buggers.

Love Life a Headache? Hot Peppers to the Rescue!

An estimated half million Americans suffer from "sex headaches" or "orgasm headaches," which tend to occur on a regular basis during or after sex. Sufferers describe it as "pulsating with a lot of pressure from the top of the head down toward the eyes," according to a study at the University of Munster. It is a relatively harmless headache with no long-term effects, but it certainly can make "getting lucky" seem ironically unlucky. Until recently, modern medicine has found no real answers regarding benign sex headaches. But there have been studies suggesting that a capsaicin (hot pepper extract) nasal spray stops and prevents sex headaches within seconds. If further studies prove this theory to be true, imagine the implications… Just add a little fuel to the fire to really get things burning.

Capsaicin spray has also been proven effective in the treatment of cluster headaches, the most excruciating form of headache known. This neuro-vascular disease, an intense and debilitating pain around one eye, strikes an estimated one percent of the world's population.

A team of researchers at the University of Florence, Italy, led by Dr. Bruno M. Fusco, treated cluster headache sufferers with a nose spray containing capsaicin for several days. During a 60-day follow-up period, eleven of the sixteen people treated reported a complete cessation of headaches. Two others reported a fifty percent reduction.

The researchers indicated that capsaicin stimulates—then blocks—a class of sensory nerve cells responsible for recognizing and then transmitting pain. One researcher observed that capsaicin "depletes the nerve endings of the chemicals which induce pain." Repeated sprayings, until the burn of the capsaicin could no longer be felt, deadened the nerves and blocked the transmission of cluster headache pain signals to the brain.

The human form as a chile pod captured in silver.

The freakiest thing about a ghost pepper is (as my mouth starts to water)—it's a very delayed burn, unlike an habanero... Burping sucks because it sends it right back to you. It's like burping hot coals.

—James Wreck of eatmoreheat.com
after eating a fresh 'Bhut Jolokia' on camera

Tasting a superhot chile gives a whole new meaning to the term "fire eater." Photo by Royce DeGrie

Chapter 14:

Superhot Stuff

Controversy surrounds superhot chiles and sauces.

People hate them. People love them. They are dangerous. They totally burn you out. They're gimmicks. They're here to stay. They're a fad. Mine's the hottest. No, mine!

See what I mean? Recently, capsaicin expert Marlin Bensinger tested some 'Bhut Jolokia' powder that was advertised as 1.6 million Scoville Heat Units. In his test with the chromatograph, the real heat was 740 thousand SHU. This kind of thing happens all the time. Testing labs all don't test to the same national standards, so tests can vary. Sometimes only one test is accepted as valid, without another test of the same material to corroborate it. Sometimes samples are submitted that are adulterated with extract, or oleoresin capsicum. This is only going to get worse as the money from the superhots increases. In a way, it will be fun to watch!

My favorite superhot experience was at a facility in Florida that bottled sauces made with oleoresin capsicum. We were shooting a segment of *Heat Up Your Life* and we needed shots of the sauce being made. So we had workers dress in total Hazmat gear that make them look like astronauts on the moon, and we faked the superhot-making by using dry ice to simulate deadly vapors.

As it turns out, our fictitious filming was frighteningly close to the truth. For example, when El Pinto Restaurant in Albuquerque was making their new Scorpion Salsa with a Trinidadian *chinense* that measured 1.21 million Scoville Heat Units, the workers were required to wear respirators, and had to cover all body parts and wear rubber gloves. Even then, the fumes got so bad that the facility had to be evacuated so it could be aired out with powerful fans. It's not nice to mess with Mother Nature, especially when it involves her hottest progeny.

> The only sauce ever banned from the Fiery Foods Show!
>
> —Slogan Dave Hirschkop used for Dave's Insanity Sauce after the banning.

What Makes Super Hot Sauces So Hot?

There are two ways to take a sauce into the upper stratosphere of heat. Sauces like Dave's Insanity Sauce contain pepper extract. Pepper extract is oleoresin capsicum, the concentrated oil containing high amounts of capsaicin. Hot peppers are dried and pelletized, then treated with hexane, which produces a dark red oily compound—the oleoresin. The oleoresin is refined to remove the oil, and the result is a crystalline powder called capsaicin. Simply put, what is happening is refining. By removing all components that are not capsaicin, you are left with pure capsaicin.

The other way is to simply use peppers that are naturally super-hot, such as 'Bhut Jolokia' (ghost peppers), 'Trinidad Scorpion', or the comparatively mild habanero.

When El Pinto developed its scorching New Mexico Scorpion Salsa for the 2010 Fiery Foods Show, workers had to wear respirators while bottling the sauce.

How Much Chile Heat is Too Much?

People vary greatly in their sensitivity to the capsaicin in chiles. Some people are so sensitive that they can get contact dermatitis from chiles touching their skin, while others can take large doses of superhot sauces with no bad reaction. But as you know, excessive consumption of many natural things (like salt) is not good for you. Some people swear by cayenne chile as an aid to circulation, and take daily capsules containing up to 60,000 Scoville Heat Units.

A Bloody Nose From Superhot Sauce

Once a reader sent in this question: "My good friend brought home some Dave's Insanity Sauce, and thought it would be good to bring it to the family BBQ. He boasted how hot it was and his mother-in-law, thinking it couldn't be that bad, soaked an onion ring in it, popped it into her mouth, and almost immediately got a bloody nose (of course followed by, 'Oh *@!%^ this stuff is hot!'). Why?"

I answered that capsaicin, the active ingredient in chiles and hot sauces, has long been thought to increase circulation. In this case, it may have increased it too much, too quickly, and caused the capillaries in her nostrils to burst. This is one of the drawbacks of the superhot sauces.

Would Eating Pure Capsaicin Kill You?

In a word, yes. Pure capsaicin is a deadly poison. Plus, it tastes like crap. However, it is useful as a repellent for roaches, mice, and other vermin, and is the active ingredient in Mace and other pepper spray.

Does Eating Super Hot Chile Burn Your Insides?

The blistering from some chiles involves people with sensitive skins or allergies, and the blistering is contact dermatitis. Studies with video endoscopy show that the lining of the stomach is not affected by the capsaicin in chiles; however, no tests have been done with super-hot sauces, to my knowledge.

What Happens When You Overdose on Superhot Chiles?

Side effects from overdosing can include burning and sometimes blistering in the mouth, light-headedness or fainting, and vomiting. I think that the superhot sauces are dangerous to people with heart conditions and breathing problems. There have been isolated cases of individuals dying after participating in superhot chile eating contests, but eating the chiles probably aggravated a preexisting medical condition like heart trouble.

How close are HPLC ratings to Scoville ratings?

Scoville ratings are based entirely upon HPLC (High-Performance Liquid Chromatography) and have been since the early '70s. No one does the Scoville Organoleptic Test any longer, which uses individuals tasting chile dilutions in controlled conditions. Why? Because it's expensive and inaccurate. HPLC accurately determines capsaicin in parts per million, which are converted to Scoville Heat Units, the industry measuring standard.

Can I Make My Own Capsaicin at Home?

All you chilehead geeks out there dreaming of setting up your own home laboratory and whipping up a bunch of capsaicin oleoresin: forget it. You need a multi-million dollar plant to do hexane extraction. Why would you want pure capsaicin, anyway? It's a deadly poison and you have to wear a full body suit to handle it.

Why Do I Feel Such a Burn With Superhot Chiles?

Superhot chiles contain massive amounts of capsaicin, which interacts with certain receptors in your mouth. Scientists Elizabeth D. Prescott and David Julius of the University of California, San Francisco, announced they had identified a lipid molecule called PIP2 that plays a crucial role in controlling the strength of the burning sensation caused by capsaicin. A lipid molecule is a fatty molecule, insoluble in water, but soluble in fat solvents and alcohol–just like capsaicin. In the mouth, there is a capsaicin receptor called TRPV1 and the lipid molecule PIP2 is bound to it. In the presence of capsaicin, the PIP2 molecule separates from the receptor, causing a painful sensation. Here's the scientific description: "In this process, the capsaicin receptor (TRPV1) is sensitized by phosphatidylinositol-4,5-bisphosphate (PIP2) hydrolysis following phospholipase C activation." That's exactly what I thought, and it's quite a mouthful.

Now, what governs the degree of pain? The strength of the binding of the molecule to the receptor, say the scientists–the stronger the binding, the more powerful the pain sensation when the capsaicin causes the separation. And what determines the strength of the binding? To quote the researchers: "Thus, modification of this PIP2 regulatory domain by genetic, biochemical, or pharmacological mechanisms may have profound effects on sensitivity of primary afferent nerve fibers to chemical and thermal stimuli under normal or pathological conditions."

Now I'm no scientist, but it seems to me that they are saying that the sensitivity to capsaicin is determined by genetics–some people's lipid molecules have a stronger bond with the capsaicin receptors than others. But by stating that biochemical and pharmacological mechanisms can also play a role, this could explain why some people become desensitized to capsaicin and can take more and more heat.

Ode to an Habanero

American chefs and cookbook authors love to wax poetic about the unique flavor of the fresh *chinense* varieties. Chef Mark Miller described fresh habaneros as having "tropical fruit tones that mix well with food containing tropical fruits or tomatoes," and Scotch bonnets as possessing a "fruity and smoky flavor." Cookbook author Steven Raichlen agreed, describing the Scotch bonnets as "floral, aromatic, and almost smoky." As far as the dried habaneros were concerned, Miller detected "tropical fruit flavors of coconut and papaya, a hint of berry, and an intense, fiery acidic heat."

Origin of the 'Red Savina' Habanero

According to Frank Garcia, Jr., of GNS Spices of Walnut, California, the hottest commercially grown habanero was developed almost by accident. Here's how it happened. Back in 1989, spice brokers had offered Frank and his partners about one-half the price they wanted for thirty acres of habaneros. Instead of dumping the crop on the market for far less than its value, the partners decided to destroy the crop by plowing it under. Just before he hopped aboard his tractor to begin the odious task, as Frank tells the tale, "I looked down and saw a strange red pepper that shouldn't be there."

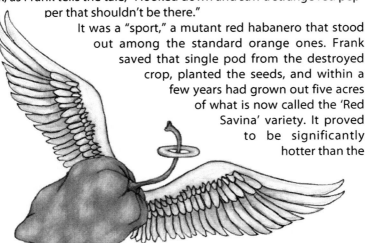

It was a "sport," a mutant red habanero that stood out among the standard orange ones. Frank saved that single pod from the destroyed crop, planted the seeds, and within a few years had grown out five acres of what is now called the 'Red Savina' variety. It proved to be significantly hotter than the

The superhot chile that started the craze—the habanero. Illustration by Lois Manno

The Outer Limits of Heat

orange pods, and Frank now has a plant variety patent on the 'Red Savina'…and the rest is history.

'Jolokia' Is a Big Hit

Ever since the Indian *chinense* variety 'Bhut Jolokia' was tested at New Mexico State University at just over one million Scoville Heat Units, it has captivated gardeners and manufacturers all over the world. It was named "Hottest Pepper in the World" by *Guinness World Records.* Danise Coon of the Chile Pepper Institute reported that the Institute sold more than 5,000 seed packets during the 2007 growing season. Several Jolokia products are now on the market. Harald and Renate Zoschke of Pepperworld.com, the leading European online hot shop, have launched Lava Jolokia Hot Sauce and Lava Jolokia Fiery Mustard. Tom and Dawn Beasley of the Montego Bay Trading Company have re-leased a 1.5-ounce shaker bottle of ground Jolokia pods and a 5 ounce "Hell's Inferno" hot sauce. Other products include "Dragon's Blood" from the U.K. and CaJohn's Nagasaurus hot sauce. Suzanne's Kitchen has just released their "Pepper Jelly Ghost," and Mrs. Renfro's Foods sells a "Ghost Pepper Salsa" to help raise funds for the Chile Pepper Institute. Undoubtedly, many more Jolokia products will soon be on the market.

Top Five Chile Plants are All Super Hot Varieties

The top seller of live chile bedding plants in the country, Cross Country Nurseries, dba ChilePlants.com, has listed their top five best selling va-rieties from 2011, and it's no surprise that superhots dominate the list.

1. 'Bhut Jolokia': This position figures because of all the super-hots, these "ghost peppers" have garnered the most publicity over the

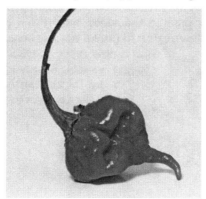 

Left: A 'Trinidad Scorpion' pod with the distinctive curved point on the end of the pod. Right: a habanero pod with the classic lantern shape. Photos by Harald Zoschke

past few years, and it doesn't seem to matter that it's been dethroned as the hottest pepper in the world.

    2. 'Trinidad Scorpion': now generally thought to be the hottest, at the upper levels measuring 1.2 to 1.4 million Scoville Heat Units. It has a better name and a more interesting pod shape.

    3. '7 Pot': A third Trinidad variety places in the top 3, showing the remarkable trend of superhots originating in the country of Trinidad & Tobago.

    4. 'Habanero Red Savina': is generally thought to be a variation on the 'Red Caribbean' varieties that are spread around the islands. It never tested as hot as 577,000 SHU in any other laboratory tests except the one that got it the Guinness record.

    5. Yellow 'Bhut Jolokia': A bit of a surprise in the number 5 position is this yellow variation of the 'Bhut Jolokia', which is becoming a favorite of chile gardeners.

German Superhot Testing

Harald Zoschke, owner of Pepperworld.com, sent some chiles to a lab in Hamburg, Germany for testing. Here are his results:

    "Our Calabrian-grown 'Bhut Jolokia' tested at 818,386 SHU (twice

'Bhut Jolokia' pods on the plant. Note the distinctive nubby texture of the pods. Photo by Harald Zoschke

the result of Assam-grown 'Bhut' analyzed at the same lab in Hamburg, btw!)

The Indians' superhot 'Chocolate Bhut' that I had tested gave only 417,888 SHU at the Hamburg lab.

This year, red 'Bhut' powder from Assam (directly from the grower/ producer) traded to Germany as having '850,000 SHU,' was tested in Hamburg and it delivered only 373,821 SHU—even some chocolate habaneros are almost that hot."

Progenitor of 'Bhut Jolokia' Found?

For the years that the rumors and then stories about the superhot 'Bhut Jolokia' from Assam in northeast India have surfaced, I've wondered about its origin. Pods of *Capsicum chinense* are found all over the Caribbean, from the Scotch bonnet in Jamaica to goat peppers in Haiti to bonney peppers in Barbados. However, it is the country of Trinidad & Tobago that seems to have the largest number of landraces of that species, including the Congo pepper, the 'Scorpion', the '7 Pot', and now the 'Jonah 7'. Of all of these, it's the Jonah 7 which most resembles the 'Bhut Jolokia', and the India connection to Trinidad is very clear: 40% of the people have an Indian ancestry, as compared to 37.5 % with an African ancestry. Marlin Bensinger, the world's foremost expert on capsaicin extraction and testing, performed HPLC tests on the 'Jonah 7', and it was in the precise heat range of 'Bhut Jolokia'. So maybe a mystery has been solved!

My esteemed colleague in Germany, Harald Zoschke, comments: "My theory is that 'Bhut' evolved from 'Fatalii' (which, of course could very well come from Trinidad, brought home to Africa by returning slaves). Now, what if 'Bhut' is a 'Red Fatalii' that trade ships brought from its home, Central Africa, to India, hundreds of years ago. And there, it just got cross-pollinated to receive the *C. frutescens* gene traces that Paul Bosland's DNA test revealed. Or maybe those genes were in the 'Fatalii' already, which a DNA test could easily prove, providing evidence for my theory. Remember, besides *C. chinense*, 'Bhut's' DNA includes 7% of *C. frutescens*. 'Fatalii' could have picked this up from Malagueta, which had spread early in Africa, becoming pili-pili or peri-peri. Also, while 'Fatalii' isn't quite as hot as Bhut, both share that intense "instant burn," as opposed to the habanero's delayed burn. Both share the poor innards, with very few seeds. Who knows, maybe all three are very closely related."

My comment back is that in this particular instance, Harald's 'Bhut' certainly does resemble a 'Fatalii', but pod variations within a landrace are common, and sometimes the pods on the same plant have different forms. This is because landraces are adapted varieties that have been growing in the same geographic area for hundreds of years, and not recently bred-to-be-true varieties. The only way to really figure this out is to compare the DNA of all these varieties.

Why Are 'Bhut Jolokia' Called "Ghost Peppers?"

Was the origin of the name Trinidadian or Indian? We probably will never know, but somehow the English name "devil" was translated into various Indian languages like Hindi and Assamese and became "ghost," or *bhut*. This is closely connected to Indian mythology and funeral practices, which hold that when a person dies, he or she leaves behind a ghost—the very rough equivalent to a Christian soul—and that ghost parallels the personality and manner of death of the deceased person. A cheerful, productive person will produce a mischievous ghost, while an evil person, or one killed violently by a tiger, will produce a ghost that turns into a demon, or devil. One source reported "Amongst the evil genii of all India, is a being called Rakshasa, of giant bulk, terrible teeth, who feasts on dead bodies. The *bhoot*, acknowledged all over India, more resembles the ghost of Europe. The Rev. Dr. Caldwell in his work on the Devil-worship of the Shanar, has shown how continuously the people of India are making new deities or de-

Twisted Pine Brewing Company in Colorado named its hot new beer after the Ghost Pepper.

The Outer Limits of Heat

mons." Another source observes, "There it is a fixed article of belief that when a man notorious for any particular vices dies, the man himself may become extinct, but his evil nature never dies, for every one of his vices then assumes personality and lives after him as a demon." In this sense, since ghosts can become devils, the words are roughly synonymous.

To prevent these ghosts from becoming demons and terrorizing the people, they take preventative action using hot peppers: "Villagers may put the peppers, incense, and other substances in a fire. The victim breathes the fumes whose effect is to smoke out the ghost." The famous mythologist Sir James George Frazier reported in his book *Psyche's Task* (1913) that "In Punjab, some people put pepper in the eyes of the corpse to prevent the ghost from seeing her way back to the house." I think the practice began with black pepper but the Indians switched to superhot chile peppers because of their superior heat, or power. And gradually, the superhot 'Bhut Jolokia' became ingrained into the culture, especially in Assam.

How Did 'Bhut Jolokia' Peppers Come to India?

It's fitting that a British Lord should be the one to carry the hottest chile pepper in the world from Trinidad to India in 1854. During a search for Caribbean Capsicums between 1700 and 1910, this quote popped up: "One species called 'devil's pepper,' introduced by Lord Harris, from Trinidad, is so intensely hot that the natives can hardly manage to use it." It was from the *Cyclopædia of India and of Eastern and Southern Asia*, edited by Edward Balfour and published in Madras, India in 1871.

My first thought: who the hell was Lord Harris? It took me only a minute to discover that he was George Francis Robert Harris, Third Baron Harris, later Third Lord Harris, born in 1810. He was among the highest elite in England, but he still had a career. He served as governor of Trinidad, and later, as governor of Madras.

An enthusiastic supporter of the Royal Botanic Gardens in Port of Spain, Trinidad, Harris lived in an era much influenced by the "Golden Age of Botany," the eighteenth century. The garden undoubtedly provided the "Devil's pepper" seeds that Lord Harris carried to India the year he left Port of Spain for Madras, 1854.

Lord Harris introduced the world to superhot chiles from Trinidad in the mid-1850s

Chilehead Resources

Scoville Heat Scale

Type of Chile	Scoville Heat Units
Pure capsaicin	16,000,000
Bhut Jolokia	1,041,427
Dorset Naga	876,000
Habanero	100,000-500,000
Chiltepin	50,000-100,000
Piquin, Tabasco	30,000-50,000
Chile de Arbol	15,000-30,000
Aji, Serrano	5,000-15,000
Jalapeño, Cayenne	2,500-5,000
Cascabel, Sandia	1,500-2,500
Ancho, Pasilla	1,000-1,500
Big Jim, Chile Powder	500-1,000
Hot Paprika, Mexi-Bell, Cherry	100-500
Pickled Pepperoncini	10-100
Mild Bell, Pimiento	0

Appendix 1:
Chile Chronology

Early Days, 1493-1607

1493, in his journal, Columbus mentions chile peppers for the first time, "There is also plenty of *ají* which is their pepper, which is more valuable than pepper, and all the people eat nothing else, it being very wholesome. Fifty caravels might be annually loaded with it from Espaniola." When he returns to Spain the same year, he brings back the first chiles to the Old World.

1519, Cortez encounters chiles in Aztec markets.

1525, Chiles reach India, which will forever change Indian food

1526, Turks conquer Hungary, bring Capsicums.

1529, Turks plant paprika at Buda (now Budapest, Hungary), establishing paprika industry.

1535, Chiles in Italy and Spain, as reported by Oviedo.

1540, Chiles in Indonesia, possibly in Germany.

1542, Three varieties of chile were on the Malabar coast of India. Chiles definitely in Germany, reported by Fuchs.

1548, Cayenne pepper was introduced into England, from India, as early as 1548, and is mentioned by Gerarde as being under cultivation in his time.

1569, Margit Szechy talks about chiles in her garden in Hungary.

1571, Francisco Hernandez sails to New Spain and begins his project to catalog all the plants of New Spain—it is the first scientific expedition to the New World. It is not published until 1628, and contains the first "recipe" ever for salsa.

1585, "Vast plantations" of chiles in Moravia, reported by Clusius.

1590, Painting of Emperor Rudolph II depicts him as Vertumnus, Roman god of abundance and uses fruits, flowers, tomatoes, maize, and chiles to form his face and torso.

1593, Clusius describes paprika.

1597, Chiles brought into what is now New Mexico by Don Juan de Oñate expedition during the founding of Santa Fe; chiles first arrive in England, mentioned by Gerard.

1604, Chile peppers mentioned for first time in Hungarian dictionary as "Turkish pepper, piper indicum."

1607, First fine art representation of tomatoes and chiles in the painting attributed to Caravaggio.

Chilehead Resources

The Middle Years, 1785-1898

1785, George Washington grows "bird peppers" and cayenne at Mount Vernon.

1794, Padre Ignatz Pfefferkorn writes about chiltepins.

1807, first bottled cayenne sauces appear in Massachusetts.

1828, J.C. Clopper describes chili con carne for first time.

1844, Josiah Gregg writes about "extravagant use" of chiles in New Mexico.

1846, L.T. Thresh names capsaicin.

1854, Governor George Harris of Trinidad takes 'Bhut Jolokia' pods and seeds to Madras, India.

1859, first "tobasco" (sic) sauce manufactured by Maunsel White.

1870, Tabasco® sauce patented by Edmund McIlhenny.

1875, Edward R. Durkee applies for a patent for "chilli sauce."

1877, Mexican cookbook lists forty-four kinds of *mole* sauces.

1888, Burpee seed catalog carries twenty varieties of chiles.

1897, New Mexico chiles transferred to Anaheim, California by Emilio Ortega.

1898, first canned chili con carne released by William Gebhardt.

The Later Years, 1912-1997

1912, Wilbur Scoville develops Scoville Organoleptic Test for chiles.

1923, Baumer Foods introduces Crystal Hot Sauce.

1917, Fabian Garcia releases 'New Mexico No. 9', the first standardized New Mexico variety.

1941, first La Victoria commercial salsa introduced.

1951, Chili Appreciation Society—International founded.

1956, *Newsweek* reports first pepper-eating contest.

1957, 'New Mexico No. 6-4' variety released, will become most famous variety.

1963, *Hungarian Paprika Through the Ages* published.

1970, Ben Villalon founds the Texas pepper breeding program at Weslaco.

1975, *The Hellfire Cookbook* published.

1977, Chili made "Official Texas State dish"; first pepper sprays introduced.

1980, *Chili Madness* published; high performance liquid chromatography for measuring chiles established by James Woodbury.

1984, *Peppers, The Domesticated Capsicums* published; *The Fiery Cuisines* published.

1987, *Chile Pepper* magazine launched.

1988, National Fiery Foods Show launched; chile breeding pioneer Roy Nakayama dies.

1990, *The Whole Chile Pepper Book* published

1996, Fiery Foods & Barbecue SuperSite launched.

1997, *Fiery-Foods & BBQ* magazine launched.

Recent Developments, 1998-2011

1998, The National Fiery Foods and Barbecue Show was the largest ever held in terms of exhibitors, with 260 in 60,000 gross square feet in the Southeast Hall of the Albuquerque Convention Center.

1999, on December 1, 1999 an Appellation d'Origine Controlee (AOC) was granted to Espelette peppers and products, giving them the same protection as more famous names, such as Champagne sparkling wine; the New Mexico State Legislature enacted a memorial making "Red or Green?" the official NewMexico State Question.

2000, worldwide pepper production tops 254,000 metric tons; the U.K. Has 8500 curry restaurants; ICS sanctions more than 300 chili cookoffs that drew more than one million people tasting, cooking, judging and having a great time; Buck Creek's Berry Hot Bar-B-Que Sauce was the Grand Prize winner in the Tasting Division at the 2000 Scovie Awards Competition.

2001, Harald and Renate Zoschke launch the Pepperworld Hot Shop in Germany, which will eventually become the largest European online hot shop.

2002, the 'Scotch bonnet' was recognized as one of Jamaica's continuing competitive non-traditional export crops; CASI sanctioned more than 500 Chili Cookoffs throughout the United States, Canada, and the Virgin Islands, and contributed over $1.2 million to worthy charitable organizations; Museo del Peperoncini— the chile pepper museum—opens about 5 miles northeast of Diamante, Calabria in the picturesque mountaintop village of Maierá.

2003, Ann Cates, an amateur jam-maker turned pro, wins the Scovie

Grand Prize, Tasting Division, for her Habanero Hula Jam.

2004, on June 26 Germany had its first Chile-Eating Championship, "Erste Deutsche Meisterschaft im Chilischoten-Wettessen"; Joe Perry of Aerosmith is featured on the January/February cover of *Fiery Foods & BBQ* magazine, the best-selling issue in the history of the magazine.

2005, the Tohato Company of Tokyo, Japan enters the Scovie Awards Competition with its habanero-spiced snacks for the first time and wins several awards.

2006, the Chile Pepper Institute was awarded the world record as the "hottest of all spices" by Guinness World Records for 'Bhut Jolokia' in September; Byron Bay Chilli Company in Australia wins the Grand Prize, Tasting Division Award for its Fiery Coconut Chilli Sauce; Garden Fresh Salsa of Michigan became the largest fresh salsa producer in the country, with sales of all products in excess of $32 million dollars.

2007, scientists prove that chile peppers were first domesticated in South America at least 6,000 years ago.

2008, Chipotle Grill's annual sales top $1.3 billion; in September, the Fiery Foods & Barbecue SuperSite has a massive redesign and expansion and takes its current look and format.

2009, FAO World Statistics for Dried Chiles & Peppers reveals that India, China, and Pakistan are the top producers, and for Fresh Chiles and Peppers the top three producers were China, Mexico, and Turkey; Dave Lutes of Hot Shots passes away.

2010, archaeological discoveries at Mayan city of Le Zotz in Guatemala included a tamale bowl with the representation of the head of a peccary; salsa sales estimated annual revenue in the U.S. market reach $158 million.

2011, for the first time in the Scovie Awards Competition's 16-year history, two products are tied for the Grand Prize in the Tasting Division: Saucy Mama Creamy Horseradish and Super Chile Toffee.

2012, Panama Red Hot Sauce wins Scovie Grand Prize; *Dave DeWitt's Chile Pepper Trivia* released at the 24th Annual National Fiery Foods & Barbecue Show.

Appendix 2:
Maximum Pungency Values
of Superhot Chiles
(as Tested in 2011)

Marlin Bensinger, an analytical chemist with his own chromatograph (two of them!) has been growing out superhots in various locations in Las Cruces and Haiti and them testing them. Here are his hottest results for the varieties he tested, except where noted, in thousands of Scoville Heat Units.

Scorpion, Butch T, Red	1,107 K
Bhut Jolokia*	1,001 K
Barrackapore	987 K
Moruga, Orange	981 K
Moruga, Red (Haiti)	952 K
Bhut Jolokia (Haiti)	941 K
Douglah	866 K
Naga Morich	837 K
Jonah 7 Pot, Red	757 K
Orange Habanero/Scorpion Cross	656 K
Chocolate Habanero	425 K
Jonah 7 Pot, Yellow	386 K
Red Savina*	249 K
Orange/Red Habanero	245 K
Scotch Bonnet	235 K
Orange Carib Habanero	225 K

*Tests by New Mexico State University

Appendix 3:
Chile Heat Scale in Scoville Heat Units (Non-Superhot Chile Varieties and Commercial Products)

Scoville Heat Units (Approximate)	Variety or Product
50,000-100,000	Santaka, Chiltepin, Rocoto, Chinese kwangsi
30,000-50,000	Piquin, Cayenne Long, Tabasco, Thai *prik khee nu*, Pakistan *dundicut*
15,000-30,000	de Arbol; crushed red pepper; habanero hot sauce
5,000-15,000	Early Jalapeño, Ají Amarillo, Serrano; Tabasco® Sauce
2,500-5,000	TAM Mild Jalapeño, Mirasol; Cayenne Large Red Thick; Louisiana hot sauce
1,500-2,500	Sandia, Cascabel, Yellow Wax Hot
1,000-1,500	Ancho, Pasilla, Española Improved; Old Bay Seasoning
500-1000	NuMex Big Jim, NuMex 6-4, chili powder
100-500	NuMex R-Naky, Mexi-Bell, Cherry; canned green chiles, Hungarian hot paprika
0-100	Pickled peperoncini
0	Mild Bells, Pimiento, Sweet Banana, U.S. paprika

Appendix 4:
Sources for Chile-related Information and Products

Dave DeWitt Picks the Top 10 Dave DeWitt Books

10. *A World of Curries* (with Arthur Pais). Little, Brown, 1994.

9. *The Southwest Table.* Lyon's Press, 2011.

8. *Barbecue Inferno* (with Nancy Gerlach), Ten Speed Press, 2001.

7. *Peppers of the World* (with Paul W. Bosland), Ten Speed Press, 1996.

6. *The Whole Chile Pepper Book* (with Nancy Gerlach) Little, Brown, 1990.

5. *The Spicy Food Lover's Bible* (with Nancy Gerlach), Stewart, Tabori & Chang, 2005.

4. *The Hot Sauce Bible* (with Chuck Evans), Crossing Press, 1996.

3. *The Healing Powers of Peppers* (with Melissa Stock and Kellye Hunter), Three Rivers Press, 1999.

2. *The Founding Foodies*, Sourcebooks, 2010.

1. *The Complete Chile Pepper Book* (with Paul W. Bosland), Timber Press, 2009.

All of my books available on Amazon.com are listed here: http://www.amazon.com/s/ref=nb_sb_noss?url=search-alias%3Dstripbooks&field-keywords=dave+dewitt&x=0&y=0

Magazine
Chile Pepper magazine, Chilepepper.com

Website and Blog
The Fiery Foods & Barbecue SuperSite, Fiery-Foods.com
Burn! Blog, Burn-Blog.com

Trade and Consumer Show
The National Fiery Foods & Barbecue Show, FieryFoodsShow.com

Professional Packaged Food Contest
The Scovie Awards Competition, ScovieAwards.com

Seeds by Mail
Chile Pepper Institute, ChilePepperInstitute.org

Bedding Plants by Mail
Cross Country Nurseries, ChilePlants.com

Ingredients and Food
Spices: TheSpiceHouse.com
Mexican: MexGrocer.com
Asian: AsianFoodGrocer.com
Thai: ImportFood.com
Caribbean: WIFGlobal.com
Indian: IndianBlend.com, ShopIndian.com
Hot Sauce: Peppers.com
Recipes: Fiery-Foods.com
Exotic Produce and Chiles: Melissas.com

Pop Quiz Answers

Chapter 7 Answers: 1, E; 2, F; 3, A; 4, C; 5, D; 6, B.

Chapter 8 Answers: 1, F; 2, E; 3, A; 4, G; 5, B; 6, C; 7, D.

Chapter 9 Answers: 1, D; 2, F; 3, A; 4, C; 5, B; 6, E.

Chapter 10 Answers: 1, C.; 2, E; 3, F; 4, A; 5, B.; 6, D.

Chapter 11 Answers: 1. H; 2. D; 3. B; 4. J; 5. A; 6. I; 7. C; 8. E; 9. F; 10. G.

Index

⭐ Please pass this
Book on 〜
Mabey another little
library box ....

CPSIA information can be obtained at www.ICGtesting.com
Printed in the USA
LVOW102112120212

268368LV00001B/3/P

9 781936 744008